SHABBAT ON WEDNESDAY

A Rabbi's Reflections on the Contemporary Scene

SHABBAT ON WEDNESDAY

A Rabbi's Reflections on the Contemporary Scene

by

MAURICE S. COHEN

KTAV PUBLISHING HOUSE INC.
NEW YORK
1976

To Rochelle

The joy of the heart is a wife

Talmud: Shabbat, 152a

CONTENTS

PREFACE

The publication of this book was motivated by the fiftieth anniversary observance of my synagogue, the Shaare Zion Congregation in Montreal.

The volume is comprised, in the main, of a selection of columns which I penned for the Congregational Bulletin down through the years. It includes, as well, a number of messages written for The Montreal Star, and an article which appeared in the Canadian Jewish Reference Book Directory on the occasion of Canadian Jewry's bicentennial celebration.

I have affixed dates to the individual pieces that the reader may be mindful of the times and issues which prompted them, and thus the better appreciate their thrust. The perspective afforded by this technique is, if nothing else, not lost upon the writer himself. For, gratifying as it is to have been proved right by the test of time, it is equally edifying to learn in retrospect where one has been wrong.

My daughter's current residency in anesthesia has led a friend to quip, "Like father, like daughter." To put people to sleep is sometimes a desirable and necessary talent, one that I have been reputed to wield in the course of my rabbinical exercises. On the other hand, I have been accused of the opposite as well, of agitating and denying *menuhah*. For the catalyst they have been in generating the fare of this volume, I must pay tribute to my congregants. For nearly thirty years I have been the recipient of both their stimulus and patience, and I realize full well how much of my own reflection is, in one way or another, a distillation of my lulling and perturbing them.

I want to record my appreciation to Mr. Emanuel Epstein, President of my congregation, and to the Board of Trustees for their large share in enabling this undertaking. I am very grateful to our Publications Committee, and especially to its Chairman, Mr. J. Harry Berger, for his consistent encouragement and valuable counsel. The cooperation and suggestions of Mr. Bernard Scharfstein of the Ktav Publishing House were of great assistance. The illustration in the book is taken from our Bulletin cover, and I wish to thank the original publisher for permission to reproduce it. I am particularly indebted to my secretary, Mrs. Mabel Usher, who not only prepared the manuscript, but helped shape it and prodded its publication.

MAURICE S. COHEN

Montreal, Quebec
November, 1975

INTRODUCTION

I shall be candid. For a rabbi, these are not kind times. Certainly there isn't abroad today that receptivity which awaited me a quarter of a century ago. The other night, typically, I was counselled against adopting a certain stance, lest I turn people off. The admonition was well-intentioned and, equally clear—not only would people disagree with me, they would turn away from me, I would lose them completely. You don't brush the accepted and popular, you don't oppose. It has been legitimized—people who don't agree don't even have to listen. This seizes me as a frightening phenomenon, a decidedly regressive development.

At its base, it is tantamount to a rank impatience and close-mindedness. Intellectual intolerance is no more kosher than religious or political intolerance. It is, to boot, self-impoverishing to shut out from one's purview ideas and views which at the moment are unpalatable. Again, it's detrimental, because it must breed falsehood and hypocrisy, an acquiescence on the part of many to violate their own inner convictions and go along, in order not to turn people off. There's an irony involved here. An age which sings loud paeans to the virtues of individualism and dissent is largely, at the same time, a generation which won't abide disagreement with it. An ambience that won't brook opposition is essentially an environment that is hostile to the democratic process itself. And, of course, it is paramountly anti-intellectual. It precludes the possibility of a rational give and take and, thus, stifles the whole climate for true objectivity. One hears only what one wants, or wills to hear. And the other side of the coin—to play it smart, one says only what wants to be heard. Honesty makes way for the agreeable and popular.

The phobia of turning people off is disfiguring the integrity of our relationships. How many parents have suddenly become sophisticated and, contrary to their own mature wisdom and experience, and abetted by the preachments of our "progressive" social scientists, have succumbed to the questionable standards of the youth culture, lest they lose all communication with the kids?

Generally today, be it to the young or to the adults, it has become wrong to moralize. You musn't register disapproval—be you a parent, or a doctor, or a teacher, or a counsellor, or a rabbi. Yours is to understand, to deal with, to treat—but you mustn't censure or moralize.

University standards and quality be damned, it is relevance that turns them on. How pathetic to see the scholar compromising his academic integrity, the writer prostituting his art—all to be popular and have a following. How ludicrous and lugubrious to behold politicians vying to be in the forefront of the new life-styles and pieties, in order to curry the favour of certain circles. How sad and repulsive to see churches and synagogues, ministers and rabbis, irresponsibly violating the essence of what they stand for, giving quarter to infantile, irreverent and freakish indulgences and "experimentations," sanctioning gross practices and even immoralities, all for the sake of being "with it" and getting a slice of the modern market.

We can't delude ourselves. The fact is that the synagogue and Judaism and the religionists at large are at odds with much that has emerged on the contemporary scene. What we must needs condemn and excoriate—the desanctification of the human being by an overly-secularized ethos, the subservience of the collectivity and public weal to an exaggerated and unbridled individualism, the insouciance of affluence, the reduction of morality to mere mores, the polarization of society, the suppression of rationality and the legitimization of violence, the burgeoning of a new and frightening mood of isolationism—is not apt to win us any popularity contests. We are in the opposition. We rub people the wrong way and bid well to estrange them.

There is no reaching here for self pity—only for a squaring with reality. And for guidance and precedent, in this pressing confrontation, I think back to what must be the lesson of the beginnings of our great Jewish history. Truth to be told, in their time, Moses and the Prophets of Israel turned our forefathers off. But in the longer run, quite patently they didn't turn them away, elsewise we would not be here as heirs of a persisting Jewish tradition which has had such a tremendous impact upon the shaping of civilization. Nay, in the more important longer run, by being honest with themselves, they even, *mirabile dictu,* turned on their people.

Perhaps if we can duplicate something of that integrity and determined insistence, and, above all, of that courage, if we are not afraid to court unpopularity and be the opposition when there is call for it—we could induce people to disagree without turning away. Perchance, we might even succeed, by the respect which our sincerity would generate and command in the longer run, in getting turned-off people turned on for God, for Torah, for Israel, and for mankind.

SPEAK UNTO THE CHILDREN OF ISRAEL

Exodus 14:2

SHABBAT ON WEDNESDAY

I appreciate the revolutionary nature of the suggestion, but I am emboldened to push it in the conviction that the general radical temper of our times has conditioned us for the far-out and off-beat. We have, indeed, become a very liberated and avant-garde generation. In a new burst of honesty and disdain for the hypocritical, we are not afraid to sunder the fetters of outworn conventionalism and empty forms. There is abroad today a spirit of openness which renders us hospitable to the most extreme changes. In an age that is eager and willing to experiment with the fundamentals of our society, I find the daring to make my suggestion. Let's move Shabbat from Saturday to Wednesday.

In a way, it means tampering with the calendar. But that should not faze us. On the contrary, it should titillate our fancy and elicit our powers of self-assertion. After all, when you get down to the bottom of things, there is no valid reason why the calendar, which is essentially just another man-made convention of yore, should hold us in its thrall more than any other humanly devised institution. Consider the experimentation that we have finally allowed ourselves with marriage and morality and the sanctity of life itself. There are no more sacred cows. If it suits our purposes and serves us better, then, by all means, let's assert our mastery over time and manipulate the calendar. Let's move Shabbat from Saturday to Wednesday.

One thing is sure. A Saturday Shabbat, in our neck of the woods, just isn't practical anymore. If I may use the verb in connection with the Sabbath, Shabbat on Saturday just doesn't work.

One has only to view the attendance at Sabbath Morning Services in almost any synagogue. Without an "occasion," congregations are very lonely and desolate places on Saturdays. There's no

3

hiding from the fact—the timing is bad. Weekends are simply no longer opportune for *shul* going. Weekends have assumed a pattern all their own. In our leisure-oriented and leisure-committed society, they are piously and religiously dedicated to the pursuit of sports and fun. Speak to a class in the Solomon Schechter Academy about participating in a Shabbat Service, and the kids are amazed at your naiveté. They are either going up to the mountains for skiing lessons or away to the country with their folks. Saturdays find families not praying together but playing and pleasuring together. No weather is too inclement to halt the hejira from the city to the slopes. And if it's not skiing, then it's tennis; and, in fairer seasons, golf. In fine, there is no time on the weekends for Shabbat and *shul.*

Wherefore, I suggest that we be realistic and come to terms with the situation. Religion is no match for leisure and pleasure, and there is no sense in beating our heads against the wall. Let's have Shabbat at a more convenient and practical time.

Wednesday strikes me as ideal. It's a midway break between the previous Sunday and the following Saturday. The Late Friday Evening Services held in some synagogues would take place on Tuesday evening, and would thus avoid conflict with the late store openings on Friday night. Sunday School can be held on Thursday afternoons. Sunday Morning Forums could assume the form of Thursday Evening Supper sessions. Day School children will be around for Wednesday Morning Sabbath Junior Congregation Services. Jewish children in the public schools? Is it any worse going to school on Shabbat, especially if it's only Wednesday, than going to ski school on Saturday? And there would even be a beneficial fallout for the observant. It would be less guilt-provoking to ride to *shul* for Shabbat Services on a Wednesday than on a Saturday.

Shabbat Shalom—a good Wednesday to you all.

February 6, 1974

AN OPEN LETTER TO THE HUMANISTS

Dear Humanists:

I read the article about your movement in the Weekend Magazine of *The Montreal Star* some weeks ago. Your views, of course, are not new to me, and, in terms of your world outlook, the piece was not too revelatory. Yet, if the article is, indeed, accurate reportage, I want to level with you and tell you that I found it no little abrasive. I gather that you are motivated to take the stance you do because of your uncompromising integrity. I respect this kind of motivation. It strikes me, however, that you are not all that honest with your children, for you are presenting them with a distorted view of theistic religion. You have every right to educate your young in your own *weltanschauung,* but it is distinctly on the unfair and dishonest side to pursue that indoctrination by misrepresenting and even defaming religious believers.

From the mouthings of your Sunday School pupils, it is apparent that you have given them the impression that religion is escapist in character and is really nothing more than an easy way out. There is no gainsaying that sometimes faith is reduced to a sort of infantile magic. Of course there are people who use their belief as a protective amulet, who take recourse to it because of fear or ignorance, who want to get off the hook and are all too ready to leave it to God. But having recognized this, surely we would be less than factual were we to present these abuses and aberrations as the real stuff of religion.

Can I commend to you for your reading a trenchant book entitled *The Individual and His Religion,* penned by the late celebrated professor of psychology Gordon Allport? Hardly a professional religionist, the author is nonetheless constrained to point out that far from being an indulgence in wishful thinking, far from being an easy way out, far from being escapist in nature, the great reli-

5

gions all demand self-abnegation, discipline, and commitment. It is not at all a realistic construction of the religious to view them as inactivists, idling their way through life, leaving it all to God. No one will seriously contend that the Prophets, for all their God-intoxication, were, vis-à-vis the social problems of their day, do-nothings. Survey our society objectively, and surely you must conclude that our conventionally religious people are not one whit less idealistic and involved in our earthly affairs than the Humanists.

On the contrary, the faithful operate under a religious obligation and compulsion to perform *mitzvot,* to do those good deeds which make this world a better world to live in. Limning, as you do, religion as an escape from human responsibility, you are either unforgivably ignorant or shamelessly defamatory.

Moreover, listening to you tell it, one would believe that you are the only ones that do any thinking. I was somewhat irritated, but even more amused, by your Ontario follower who, accusing the local clergy of having a stake in the status quo, allows: "But we have upset their comfort. We make them feel insecure by making them think a little." It was this kind of strutting that provoked the late philosophical Rabbi Milton Steinberg to remark in his essay on *The Common Sense of Religious Faith:* "It is not true, as the agnostic claims, that only his position is consistent with intellectual integrity. For, as we shall soon discover, the evidences for the religious outlook are more than adequate to justify a decision in its favor. Mental honesty is no monopoly of anyone, let alone of those who refuse to make up their minds."

If you Humanists are persuaded that your reason leads you to believe that there is no God, or that God is irrelevant, do not convey to your children the unwarranted arrogance of denying that other people's reason leads them to posit the existence and relevance of God. It's nothing short of infantile snobbery to feel that atheism is a reasoned stance and that theism is an unreasoned position. At the very least, the God thesis is a wholly reasonable, rational and logical assumption. Indeed, speak of thinking, and I am compelled at this juncture to turn the tables on you. It is Humanism that is far too arbitrary and limited in its ratiocination. Not only are we willing to think, but we tend to think more deeply and more daringly than you.

I have no illusions about converting you to my point of view. But please, in pursuing your own ideology, be honest with your children and don't give them any distorted impressions of religion and religious people.

January, 1968

IT'S TOUGH TO BE RELIGIOUS

Religion is for softies.

This is not an uncommon asseveration, and perhaps you yourself have at times shared in something of that evaluation. The persuasion is that people who are riddled with fear or steeped in superstition, people who haven't the inner fortitude to face and negotiate the realities of life on their own, who require a crutch on which to lean—softies of this ilk need religion. As someone put it to me unabashedly the other day, "You have to be weak to be religious."

To tell the truth, I've never considered myself to be a stalwart. On the other hand, I don't exactly fancy being told that my adherence to religious faith indicates that I am a *nebech*, a weakling. Indeed, when I think upon it, I am constrained to conclude that the opposite is the case—that whatever else it calls for, it takes the stuff of strength to be religious. And I should like to reject the broadside that is levelled at us religious folk from securalist quarters and put the record straight. On the contrary, you have to be strong to be religious.

For one thing, religion requires intellectual puissance. It is rooted in the potency of an uncompromising ratiocination, in the strength of an insisting logic, in the energy of an undeterred probing, in the daring of mental venture. There is no refuting the contention that God is not scientifically verifiable. If I have intellectual guts, however, I'll refuse to accept the limits on my reasoning set by the materialists. To confine all reality to the provable and refuse to probe beyond the physical fare of our existence is, in my sight, a lazy, an arbitrary, an unjustified approach. The fact is that my mind, as does yours, insists upon digging deeper and asking for a thesis which will rationally explain the mystery of life. If you are not afraid to loose the fetters of conventional scientific knowledge, if there courses in you an overpowering reason, you will have to reckon with a God hypothesis. The primary tenets of religion are not the result of any softness. They are the consequence of intellectual vitality and cogency.

It takes strength to be religious, in the second instance, because you have to be strong enough to subject yourself to a system which is inordinately demanding of your person, a regimen of self-abnegation, discipline and surrender. There is no faith which is not inextricably tied up with a restrictive and inhibiting code of behavior, both of a ritual and ethical caliber. No one can seriously deny that it takes more inner fortitude, call it character, to live by a code than to live impulsively or by the convenience of situational ethics.

Moreover, religion is for the toughies because it nastily denies us the ease of anonymity. Instead of allowing us the comfort of losing ourselves in the crowd, it focuses on the individual. More than any other system, it invests us with onerous personal responsibility. "For me the world was created" is its conviction, in the sense that I am answerable for the shape of things. Would that I could be part of the band wagon, inconspicuous and in stream with the indiscriminately changing times, or, at least, free to do as I choose in my own private affairs. But my commitment doesn't give me that out. Instead it challenges me with duty and disturbs me with guilt for the ills of the world.

Religion is for softies? That's fuzzy thinking. You have to be strong to be religious.

December, 1970

IT HAS SOMETHING TO SAY

Whether or not religion is revealed is not as significant as the fact that it is revelatory. The important point for the nonce is, not so much that our faith is the result of a revelation, but rather that there is a revelation in our faith, that in it there is something relevant for life which can be found nowhere else.

By and large, the modern mentality denies this. It rejects the thesis that religion has something exclusive to disclose and impart to us. Laplace bespoke the contemporary *shtimmung* when he asserted that "God is a hypothesis I can do without." One doesn't need the God thesis anymore to explain the physical universe. Science is many times more revealing and illuminating in this area. The ethical life? By now it's our conviction that man himself is the measure of all things, and that human intellect and reason are the best source and guide for the moral life. For our intellectualized age, not only is religion not revealed; more pointedly, it has nothing to reveal. It is quite irrelevant and superfluous.

I have a charming little book which is comprised of letters written to God by small children. An epistle from a young lady to the Lord runs as follows: "Dear God, Are you real? Some people do not believe it. If you are, you better do something quick. Harriet Ann." Taking a good honest look at the shape of things in our advanced milieu, I wonder if God is not doing something to confirm His reality. Considering the nature of the "beautiful" new world we have shaped with sheer intellect, are we really convincd that religion has nothing to reveal to us?

Wishful thinking won't make it otherwise. If there is any patent fact which emerges out of the contemporary scene, it is this: there is in man a wild and animalistic streak, and reason alone is not adequate to curb and control it. Let's face it—intellectually, morality doesn't have a leg to stand on. It is no accident that, shorn of its

10

religious underpinnings, our culture has soured and turned into filth. It is precisely the intelligentsia in the worlds of literature, the theater, and the campus who are purveying immorality as the new-morality of our emancipated age.

Eric Hoffer's observation is frightening but pungent. We have yet to assimilate the fact, he states, that it took a nation of philosophers to produce Hitler and Nazism and that the Stalin cult was the work of intellectuals. He uses a phrase that is altogether too meaningful for us—"tyranny by an intellectocracy." Analyze it, honestly, and more often than not the approach of confrontation that is so zealously espoused by our modern young crusaders is virtually the doctrine of might makes right. If peace is in any wise an integral part of ethics, does not the use of violence in the internal affairs of our society clearly make us something less than moral?

"They that deny a God, destroy man's nobility," wrote Francis Bacon; "for certainly man is of kin to the beast by his body, and be he not kin to God by his spirit, he is a base and ignoble creature." How revealing—Laplace, who didn't need God in his scheme of things, wrote toward the end of his days: "I have lived long enough to know what I did not at one time believe—that no society can be upheld in happiness and honor without the sentiment of religion."

Religion superfluous and irrelevant? Hardly. Whether or not religion is revealed, it harbors a revelation for mankind.

May, 1969

DON'T TRIVIALIZE YOUR FAITH

Sometimes our fault is not estrangement, but rather insufficiency. We're involved, but we give the matter less than it requires.

There is a book on the market called *The Overweight Society*. In reviewing the book, Cleveland Amory was reminded of a passage which runs as follows: "Ask God to show you why you eat too much, ask God to attend each bite, ask God to help you exercise, and ask God to help you face this hard fact: all your life you'll be fat-prone." Asking of religion too much, when you would use it as a diet pill? On the contrary, it's asking too little. When you would employ religion as a crutch, your approach is less than the matter merits.

We snicker, sophisticates that we are, when someone suggests religion for losing weight. But in principle we're not beyond that sort of thing ourselves. John Gunther once said, "I believe we are all part of a universe that has certain forms, patterns, interrelations and compensations, even for the worst of personal tragedies. And, if things go wrong the concept of God not only can give us hope and succor, it also relieves us of some responsibility. Of course I believe in God." I go along with Mr. Gunther to a point. But surely the relief which religious faith brings us from personal responsibility, as we face the harsh realities of life, should not be the primary reason for our believing in God.

Rabbi Moses Loeb of Sasov, a mystic of the last century, was asked by one of his disciples, "Why did God create the quality of skepticism?" And the good rabbi answered, "That thou mayest not let the poor starve, putting them off with the joys of the next world, or simply telling them to trust in God who will help them— instead of supplying them with food."

Gott vet helfen, "God will help"—that can of course be the very salt of the deepest religious faith. On the other hand, it can also be, as I'm afraid it very often is, scarcely more than a convenient crutch to get you off the hook. You are needed, your help is called for—and suddenly you wax religious and leave it all to God. To be sure, there are instances when only God will help. George Eliot once observed: "We hand folks over to God's mercy, and show none ourselves." When religion becomes that kind of crutch in our scheme of things, when we use it to coast by on God's power instead of employing our own energies, we are giving religion less than it demands.

We bring our religion less than it deserves when we deny it the dimension of rationalism. In the bifurcation of reality into the realms of reason and emotion, too often there is the proclivity to assign faith almost exclusively to the latter. This is true, mind you, not only on the part of the untutored whose propensities are naturally for the anti-intellectual, but on the part of intellectuals themselves who have some or a great deal of affinity for the spiritual life. There is a kind of piegon-holing, a kind of compartmentalization, that is involved here. Science, politics, economics, sociology, disciplines of this sort belong within the sphere of rationalism and consequently must meet the criteria of reason; but art, literature, and especially religion transcend the rational, and, for the likes of them, the criteria are primarily a matter of feelings and not reason. The result is that there has emerged the attitude that religion need not and, indeed, can not be evaluated in terms of reason. In the more extreme expressions of this attitude, the conviction is that the more irrational it is the more profoundly religious it is. And so there is distilled in our midst an ambience of mysticism, as if the path to real religion is exclusively by way of our emotional apparatus and has nothing to do with our rational faculties.

On a less sophisticated level, this phenomenon is exemplified in the oft-expressed dichotomy between belief and thought—as if one has nothing to do with the other! Said a minister to his congregation in the course of his sermon on the need for greater faith, "Don't, my dear friends, put me down as a thinker; put me down as a believer." I grant you that this kind of an attitude is more apt to be found in non-Judaistic faiths than in our own. But the fact is that we are not free from such obscurantist indulgences.

I speak to Jewish scientists, and suddenly, as if an iron curtain is dropped, their scientism has no bearing whatsoever upon what they believe. As one of them put it to me, these are two separate worlds. Dr. Trude Weiss-Rosmarin has on several occasions noted the phenomenon of large numbers of Jewish boys and girls who refuse to attend college and reject their exposure to any kind of education or knowledge other than religious. Our own community is not without a sampling of this religious anti-intellectualism.

No one wants to denigrate the role of emotion in faith nor dismiss cavalierly the intuitive insights of mysticism. But surely, if religion is part of our world, then it cannot arbitrarily divorce itself from the realm of the rational. Faith may transcend the reaches of reason, but it cannot contravene reason, it cannot be irrational and still command validity. More than that, belief without thinking can too readily become sheer fantasy and superstition.

In riposte to Schleiermacher's emphasis upon feeling as the basic element in religion, Hegel exclaimed, "Aber das Denken ist auch Gottesdienst"—"But thinking is also worship." When we fail to think and reason about faith, we accord our religion less than it deserves.

October, 1967

A FACULTY OF KOSHER CATERING

Dr. Gerson Cohen,
Chancellor,
Jewish Theological Seminary,
New York City

Dear Dr. Cohen:

There ought to be a new department of studies at the Seminary.

You have, no doubt, heard of the young man who started out to become a minister, but then changed his mind and became, of all things, a jockey. His friends said of him that he succeeded in bringing more people to contrition in that profession then he would have as a clergyman.

I don't know about bringing people to contrition, but I certainly feel that it is our aim to bring more people to *shul*. And I'm not at all convinced that the training of rabbis is the most effective method of achieving that end.

What about producing, instead, caterers?

I mean that literally, and not figuratively. To be sure, rabbis ofttimes feel that they are in the catering business. Ostensibly there to serve the needs of their people, in actuality they end up catering to the whims and fancies of their congregants and communities. You and I appreciate the difference between "needs" and "desires," between "serving" and "catering." But that frustration aside for the moment, I mean "catering" in the most conventional connotation of that term, in the sense of catering food.

Our local press frequently carries ads sponsored by a highly traditional Jewish movement aimed at attracting college youth. Prominently featured in the advertisements is an invitation to a free delicious Shabbat evening meal. From my reading of colleagues' bulletins, I note that more and more Late Friday Evening

15

Services are being replaced by Friday Evening Dinners in the synagogue. I hear tell of congregations that attract hundreds of worshippers, whole families, every Sabbath morning with their sumptuous "hot kiddushim." We shouldn't sneer at this. The way to a man's heart, after all, including his Jewish heart, may very well lie via his stomach. Forgive the indelicate pun—a gutsy Judaism.

There is a hitch here. Food today is a very expensive item. Can the average congregation afford such a tack? I wouldn't want my *baale-batim* to hear me say this, but, if I were the president of a *shul*, I would push for dispensing with rabbinical costs and investing the savings in a real good catering program. I don't for one moment underestimate my own abilities. I don't, however, delude myself—for a steady diet, I am not nearly as delectable and attracting with my spiritual nourishment as is a caterer with his culinary fare. My mouth waters at the thought of what congregations could do food-wise with their rabbinical budgetary allocations.

Sooner or later, our laymen are going to come to this realization on their own. The average *shul* can benefit more from a caterer than it can from a rabbi.

This does not mean that we don't need rabbis anymore. That's not true. Only, we can do with a good deal fewer of them. Just two or three in the community at large—to look after the marriages and burials and pastoral services. But as for the *shuls*, the many *shuls* in the community, they will all need kosher and skillful resident caterers. That's where the real dearth lies.

Wherefore, I am taking this liberty of turning to you and the Seminary and suggesting that you institute a new department of studies for Congregational Catering. In the past, the Seminary proved itself non-pareil in the area of Torah. I am confident, in meeting the challenge of the hour, it can become equally enriching in the domain of *kemach*.

Respectfully yours,
Maurice S. Cohen

February, 1975

FROM CREATURES TO CREATORS

"Man is made to create, from the poet to the potter." So wrote Disraeli more than a century ago.

In more recent times, Eric Fromm has sought to give this creative urge wherewith we are informed an explanation in depth. "Man," he writes, "is thrown into this world without his knowledge, consent or will, and he is removed from it again without his consent or will. In this respect he is not different from the animal, from the plants, or from inorganic matter. But being endowed with reason and imagination, he cannot be content with the passive role of the creature. . . . He is driven by the urge to transcend the role of the creature, the accidentalness and passivity of his existence, by becoming a creator . . . In the act of creation, man transcends himself beyond the passivity and accidentalness of his existence into the realm of purposefulness and freedom."

In this vein, I am prompted to ask what is our role vis-à-vis our Jewishness. Is it creative or is it passive?

When the late Justice Brandeis was at Harvard, he was the first Jew chosen to become a member of a certain honor society in that university. In his acceptance speech, Brandeis opened by saying, "Gentlemen, I am sorry I was born a Jew. I wish I could have chosen it."

It's not enough to be born a Jew. Just that, just a Jew by accident of birth—that's too passive, that's unsatisfying. There is in us an urge for a more active and creative role. We want to share in making and determining our Jewishness. And this we can do. We can gratify that drive by playing a more telling and more creative role in every phase of our Jewishness; by allowing nothing Jewish just to happen to us but rather by insisting on having a moulding hand in all that is part of Jewish life.

Nowhere are you and I afforded a more rewarding opportunity

17

to exercise our Jewish creativeness than within the framework of that institution which goes to the core of Jewish living, the synagogue. The synagogue is not, as we are sometimes wont to envisage it, just a preserver of a heritage which has been bequeathed to us out of the past. It is rather an instrument whereby we, who participate in it actively, fashion a distinct mode of living for the present and shape the destiny of our children and future generations.

It is through the synagogue that we create our own awareness of God and remain not merely the passive recipients of a nebulous conventional belief. It is through the synagogue that we take a tradition not fabricated by our own hands and, bringing it to bear on the contemporary scene, distil values and guidance for modern society. It is paramountly through the synagogue that we transform the old story of Jewishness into an exciting and challenging raison d'être for Jewish survival. As Jews, we have not by a long shot completed our contribution to civilization. We have yet a great deal to offer mankind, and this we shall do above all else when we again become a religiously creative people.

It is abundantly patent that Israel is central in the whole texture of Jewish creativity. The establishment of that State twenty-two years ago was one of the great watersheds in our chronicles and is destined to play a telling role in the shaping of Jewish and even world history. To the extent that a Jew can hew his own fate and influence the course of human civilization to come, he must be an integral part of the Israel story.

We have the potentiality for freedom. Let's not stifle it. We can transform ourselves from Jewish creatures into Jewish creators.

March, 1970

BETWEEN THE LINES OF PRAYER

Why should you worship?

There are many reasons. I want now, however, to focus on a few basic motivations. To begin with, if you believe there is a God, then you ought to declare and publicize that conviction. And indubitably, the best way of making known your belief in God is by way of worship. Every time you go to *shul* to a service, you are virtually asserting to your milieu that, for all your theological uncertainties and confusions, your bet is that there must be a Deity.

We ought to declare and publicize this belief which lies deep in us for the reason that it's the kind of big idea that needs out from our narrow encapsulated selves and begs for sharing with others. Again, we ought to dramatize this internal faith of ours for the reason that those who are in the opposite camp and are sure that God is dead are making a lot of noise which we must counter. In a sense, worship is the way we demonstrate against the secularization of our time and for a theistic reading of life.

Secondly, worship transforms God from an impersonal intellectual datum into a living reality. It creates an avenue of communication between the Divine and us. When you pray, you distil a sense of relationship to the Divine which uniquely engenders a sense of personal significance. And if I gauge the contemporary condition correctly, nothing does man lack and need as much as a feeling of personal worth. The technological character of our society, coupled with the bigness of everything, has in effect gone a far way in depersonalizing the human being and in deracinating his self-esteem.

"Jones," thundered the office autocrat at his brow-beaten employee, "I understand you've been going over my head!" The timid fellow murmured that he hadn't said anything to anyone as far as he knew. "Don't lie," snarled the boss. "Isn't it true that you have

19

been praying for a raise?" There's more than humor in the tale. When you pray, you put yourself in no less than a speaking relationship with God, you rub elbows with the Divine. You become somebody all over again.

Finally, I have no statistics on the matter and cannot document the correlation between ritual and morality. I admit there are those who worship and who, ethically, are not all that they might be. But whether a person is more honest because he goes to *shul* is not at the moment important. What is significant and what is so telling in this whole situation is the fact that you expect such a person to be more honest. When you worship, you put yourself visibly on the spot, you openly commit yourself to higher standards, you expose yourself to a moral challenge. If they are not necessarily more ethical, people who sit in the pews at least distil a greater awareness of ethics than those who don't sit in any pews. When you worship, you keep alive an ethical expectancy.

October, 1968

THE FALLACY OF JEWISH HUTZPAH

A sense of shame is a nuclear and inseparable part of Jewishness.

So convinced of this were our Sages, that they aver in the Talmud that, "He who is not shamefaced—it is certain that his ancestors were not present at Mount Sinai." Whatever else it did by way of molding the Jewish character, that seminal confrontation between God and Israel thirty-one hundred years ago, celebrated by the Shavuot Festival, imprinted on the Jewish soul a sense of shame. Jewish *hutzpah* may be proverbial; in the authentic traditional purview, however, its antipode, *boshet panim*, shamefacedness, is far and away more cardinally Jewish.

A sense of shame. What does it signify?

To start with, it bespeaks a fundamental humility. When I suffer embarrassment, it indicates that I am measuring and evaluating myself by a criterion which transcends my parochial person. When I am ashamed, it's obvious that I am not so arrogant as to make my own rules and call the game as I alone see fit.

Secondly, shamefacedness is more than modesty—it's a feeling of responsibility, a sense of obligation, a conviction that one ought to live up to and be in consonance with certain standards of the broader reality. If I didn't feel I ought to be or do better, then why would I be bothered by the barb of inferiority? Essentially, shamefacedness is my responsiveness to challenge, my subserviance to the ethical dictate.

And thirdly, it's a commitment to optimism, or at least, meliorism. It's only because deep down in my bones I appreciate that I don't have to settle for what I am and for how I behave, it's only because I realize that I can change and be different, that I feel ashamed. It's the kind of virtue which is rooted in the optimistic base of potentiality. I don't but I really should, and can—that's what makes me ashamed.

Add it all up, and it amounts to this—the sense of shame is the moral catalyst par excellence. Solomon Ibn Gabirol, the great medieval Jewish philosopher and poet, understandably rates it as the chief of all the ten virtues.

To be shamefaced may be moral and noble, but there is no hiding the truth that it's hardly comfortable and pleasant. At the very least, it is disturbingly and frustratingly inhibitive. How to avoid the nagging and pressure of shame? One way, of course, is to eschew the behavior which breeds guilt. But that's difficult. An easier way is to stifle the sense of shame.

You can, for example, blind yourself to those realities which would make your juices of guilt and remorse run. Or, you can go through certain gestures of piety, and ritualize your way out of the squeeze of conscience. Or again, you can use the good old standby of the alibi and facilely dig up a good excuse for your failure. Nowadays, however, the most common and most effective method employed for stilling a sense of shame is exercising something akin to *hutzpah*. You play the sophisticate and consciously steel yourself not to be upset. You consciously assume a mien of unadulterated brazenness. You take the stance that you're going to be "mature" and "honest" and not give a damn.

And so, *mirabile dictu*, we have become one of the most "honest" of generations. Courtesy is so much pretense and facade; we opt for the "honesty" of being rude and vulgar. Young people are too truthful to be curbed by factitious filiality; they seek to be "honest" and tell their parents and elders off. Reserve and self-respect are the stuff of prudishness; artists today prefer to be "honest" and pornographic, the public "mature" and voyeuristic. It's a sham to get hung up on moral taboos; one should be "mature" enough to come to grips with one's sexuality. Jewish ignorance is hardly a new phenomenon; but today people are "open" about it and are unashamedly Jewish ignoramuses. See how "honest" some of us have become—Jewish youth, propelled by a burst of universalism, are not diffident about siding with the enemies of Israel, and can, with equanimity, seek the destruction of their own people.

Shamefacedness, allowed the Sages, is a legacy we inherited along with the Decalogue from that revolutionizing encounter of ours at Mount Sinai. When you think on it, there can be no Ten Commandments where there is no sense of shame.

May, 1971

WHEN YOU DON'T FEEL LIKE IT

It's no good unless it comes from within you.

You've heard this sentiment expressed so many times, in this guise or in its galaxy of variations. Perhaps you've even had occasion to utter it yourself. When your heart's not in it, isn't it meaningless to pursue the task, and even hypocritical? Genuineness is a matter of inner conviction and we are less than sincere when the spirit doesn't move us.

But suppose now that it doesn't come from within you, suppose that your heart isn't in it. What's the implication? Better not to do it at all? If you have to be pushed and coerced, then it's senseless and preferable to desist altogether? I appreciate that that is the prevalent sentiment today. Be true to yourself, don't be a hypocrite; be honest and do only what you want to do.

To be sure, conviction is very important. Sincerity is irrefragably one of man's finest virtues. But when the spirit is not there, we would do well to proceed anyway. I'm suggesting that if we can't act out of conviction, we ought at least to act out of duty. More often than not, what is begun as a duty blossoms into conviction and inner commitment. The many things you feel like doing today, did they all stem from your personal inclination, or perchance were some of them initiated by one pressure or another? There is no denigrating the worth of conviction, but neither should we underrate the value of duty.

You don't feel like reading, literature is not your cup of tea. In no wise do I want to encourage dilettantism. Playing at culture is not the point. There is, however, the distinct possibility that if, to begin with, you compel yourself to seek improvement and expose yourself to the realm of literature, before long there will be generated in you a genuine proclivity for reading. What was begun out of a sense of duty insinuates itself into your very fabric and becomes a source of pleasure.

I find this to be the case so often in the instance of Jewish studies. People will enroll in a course out of self-compulsion or external persuasion, almost convinced that this is not for them; and they are amazed to find, with the passing of time, that Jewish learning can be pleasurable and that they have even developed a desire for it. Perhaps someone reading this column is a principled absentee from our Sabbath Services. It's not in his heart to worship, and to go through the mechanics would be so much hypocrisy. It is true, Tradition underscores the importance of inner conviction in prayer. But if that genuine motivation is not there *ab initio*, perhaps we can allow obligation to propel us and develop in us the appropriate spirit.

This is the season in which we celebrate the concept of Brotherhood. What should you do, however, when because of something in you or in your neighbor, you don't feel like being a brother? When you don't feel like it, be a brother nonetheless. You may be surprised; before long you may discover that your heart's in it.

February, 1966

A REQUIEM FOR KADDISH

Kaddish Judaism!

Most of us are aware of what this phrase connotes. It's a Judaism that eerily focuses almost exclusively on observances that are connected with death. Except for the High Holy Days, he never set foot in *shul;* but now he is there morning and evening saying *kaddish* for his deceased parent. When the prescribed period terminates, we will not again see him so soon. Forgive me, he'll be around at *yizkor* time and for the *yahrzeit,* too. There are so many facets to our Judaism, really lively and important *mitzvot,* which beg for our constant devotion and ongoing commitment. Yet here is a Jew whose connection with his faith is so infrequent and occasional—and so morbid to boot. Objectively viewed, no one will blame us if we are rather disdainful of this kind of hollow religiousness. There is something terribly dead about *kaddish* Judaism.

But wait now, let's not be such smug perfectionists. The truth of the matter is that even *kaddish* Judaism is dying. The truth of the matter is that it's the rare son who appears in the synagogue during the mourning period to recite the *kaddish* for the loss of a parent. We are fast becoming mathematical geniuses today. Somehow we've even found a way to transpose the "shivah" (which literally means seven) into a three-day observance. It becomes more and more discernible in the synagogue as the years roll on —the heretofore traditional *yizkor* "crowd" is thinning out and is no longer such a crowd. Patently, the memorial service no longer has the magnetic power to elicit our resolve to overcome every difficulty and be there.

We have what I feel is a meaningful custom in our synagogue. At our Sabbath Morning Service, we recite a special prayer in memory of the deceased whose *yahrzeits* will be observed during the forthcoming week. We ask the families of those memorialized to

25

make it a point to be with us on that occasion. Many do come. No little disconcerting is the fact, however, that many don't. People are not so meticulous about *yahrzeits* any more.

I suppose that in large measure the death of *kaddish* Judaism is part and parcel of the overall decline of religious observance. We would be willfully blind were we to shut our eyes to the creeping secularization of our times. We believe less and less, and so we overlook more and more. But it's not only religious sacrilege that's involved in the passing of *kaddish* Judaism. Let's be frank about it. Many of those who used to observe were not so motivated by considerations of faith as they were by reverence for their dear ones. This was always present—a respect for the memory of their parents.

Lamentably, we must conclude that not only has our religious faith waned, but so too has our *kibbud horim,* our honoring of parents, lessened. The fact is we are not so willing today to go out of our way for their sake and memory. Is it possible that something of this alienation has been conveyed to our own offspring? I mean, should we really be shocked by the irreverence and lack of respect of our young when it is altogether likely that we pave the way and show them the example?

Don't scorn it. There's a lot to be said for *kaddish* Judaism.

November, 1967

CREDENTIALS FOR PREACHING

"Who are you to tell me?!"

Such was the question wherewith I was confronted in a discussion with a group of young people during the past High Holy Days season. The allusion was to the validity of the sermon. The candor and honesty that prompted the query took the edge off its impertinence, and I therefore felt no offense. The young man was merely voicing a sentiment that rankles in the minds of many of his peers today. It's just another aspect of the overall questioning of authority which pervades the contemporary *zeitgeist*. What gives a rabbi the right to stand at his pulpit and "tell" people?

To begin with, the question betrays an unfounded preconception. It is not the intention of the rabbi in his sermon to "tell" people. The authoritarianism suggested by that verb is simply not there and is unfairly imputed. The aim in the synagogue discourse is not to order and command; but rather to observe, to share an opinion and an idea, possibly even to inform and to teach. The rabbi merely wants to "talk" to his people, wants to communicate with them. Perhaps no one more than he is aware of the current alienation sired by the lack of communication. He, on his part, desperately wants to relate and get through. But whatever else communication entails, it requires the readiness of people to listen.

True. One should listen. But why *davka* listen to the rabbi? What gives him the privilege of commanding attention? At the very least, the selfsame privilege to be heard that is enjoyed by every individual. We ought to listen to everyone, including the rabbi. Common courtesy dictates no less an openness for what he has to say than that which is accorded to anyone else.

And perhaps even a greater openness. There are no illusions here that the rabbi is an expert on every subject which he treats from the pulpit. He is cognizant of the fact that there are those who are far more qualified than he to deal with the matter at hand. He lays no claim to special authority every time he speaks. On the other hand, a sermon does represent a measure of preparation, of researching, of deliberation and thinking-the-thing-through that the average person in his audience has either not had the opportunity to invest or taken the pains and time to exercise. The sermon may not be authoritative, but neither is every editorial or essay, which, nonetheless, can be eminently rewarding and worthwhile. When the rabbi speaks from the pulpit, he's not talking off the top of his head, and deserves to be heard.

Besides, let's divest ourselves of false humility. Wide-roaming as the sermon may be, more often than not it has a particular objective—to bring to bear the religious Jewish point of view. To indulge a popular term nowadays, it seeks Jewish relevance. And in this sphere, the rabbi, by virtue of his commitment and education and training, and by virtue of his very vocation, is more qualified and better equipped. He does possess an authority, an earned authority, that others do not. He does operate with a kind of expertise, a kid of specialty, that is singular and rarely the advantage of his listeners. He is a professional, and as such merits attention.

"Who are you to tell me?" I don't necessarily want to "tell" you anything. I only want to talk to you. And just because I am a rabbi, you don't have to be perverse and shut me out.

November, 1970

A CONGREGATION MAKES A RABBI

A congregation doesn't engage a rabbi.

A long time ago the Sage Joshua ben Perahya counselled us, *Aseh lecha rav,* "Make for yourself a rabbi." That's what a congregagtion does—it doesn't find, it doesn't import, it doesn't employ; it makes a rabbi. Everyone knows that a congregation can break a rabbi. It's more important to appreciate that a congregation makes a rabbi.

How?

To begin with, by being just that, a congregation. A congregation is not a synagogue. A synagogue is a building, a membership list, a communal institution. A congregation, on the other hand, is people—someone you can talk to, living human beings who can hear you, someone you can teach and counsel, someone you can criticize and scold, someone you can commend and compliment. A congregation above and beyond everything else is people. You make him a rabbi when you present him, not with a synagogue, but with a congregation.

A rabbi is not infallible. We have no doctrine of infallibility in Judaism. There will be times when the rabbi is wrong, and you don't have to listen to him. You don't have to listen to him, but you have to hear him out. This much you owe a spiritual leader —to hear him out. And when you disagree with him, as is your prerogative, you ought to disagree with reverence and respect. Our tradition insists that *derech eretz,* courtesy, even takes precedence over Torah. If you want Torah, if you want a rabbi, then you must needs first create an environment of *derech eretz.* A congregation makes him a rabbi when it accords him proper regard and reverence.

You make him a rabbi, too, when you encourage him to study, when you allow him the time to be away from congregational affairs and duties for regular appointments and meetings with his books. Indeed, the essential meaning of his title *rav* is "teacher." When the Sage Joshua suggested that we make for ourselves a rabbi, he was in fact advising us to make for ourselves a teacher. Give him the opportunity to teach you; ask of him, demand of him Jewish instruction—and you will make him a rabbi.

I once heard tell of an individual who resigned from a club saying, "I don't want to belong to any society that would accept me as one of its members." There is no hinting here at any policy of exclusiveness; and certainly a congregation is not a club. We are, however, asking for standards. A congregation has to have character.

I was saddened no end by the admission of a young colleague. In a confessional mood he allowed that if he were to leave the rabbinate, he would never become a member in his congregation. That's about as withering a commentary on a congregation as one can ever hear. Make sure by virtue of your demeanor as a congregation, by the ethics and pattern of your behavior, that you are the kind of congregation your rabbi would join were he a layman. You make him a rabbi when you are a congregation with standards.

I salute a congregation that makes rather than employs a rabbi.

October, 1968

THE ADVANTAGES OF THE DIRECT APPROACH

It's no great shakes to be a *shaygetz*.

That's what we call the individual who, unabashedly and without compunction, is not afraid to be direct and come right out with it to your face. A *shaygetz*. This Yiddishism betrays the innate delicacy and sensitiveness of the Jewish soul. Even though it's the truth, you don't, without diffidence and without regard for his feelings, tell anybody off. *Areinzogen*, giving it to him straight —this is not for a Jew. To do that, you have to be a *shaygetz*, a pagan.

It's no great shakes to be a *shaygetz*. But neither is its antipode in any wise praiseworthy. I don't like the fellow who all too brazenly lets me have it straight from the shoulder. However, I am not less afraid of the individual who has something to say to me, yet, for one reason or another, is furtive and shies away from me. There is much to be said for the direct approach. One doesn't have to be a *shaygetz* in order to be truthful and use the direct approach. There is telling and telling. And, as Disraeli once remarked, "There is no wisdom like frankness."

The direct approach is a sagacious course because it keeps us from falling victim to three snares.

In the first place, it prevents us from nursing and building up a grievance in our heart which can only generate hostility. The longer a resentment is locked away in your person and not released, the longer you eschew communicating your sentiment to the party involved, the more intense will that animosity grow. When we don't use the direct approach, we are very apt to distil hatred.

Secondly, more often that not, the critique we hesitate to offer directly we communicate instead to others. Instead of talking to the party, we talk about him; instead of *rayden*, we *ba-rayd*. You don't tell him, but you tell the whole world. The fact is, it's almost impossible to keep sentiments locked up in oursleves. When we can't be straightforward with an individual, very often we end up not only disliking him, but viciously getting everyone else to dislike him. The direct approach has the virtue of diminishing the inclination to gossip and slander.

And thirdly, evasiveness precludes the opportunity for dissipating the antipathy. You know this from your own experience. Very often, after you've talked it over, somehow the grievance lifts and disappears. Perhaps it's an explanation that changes the whole complexion of the situation and attenuates the feelings. Perhaps it's a show of contrition and genuine regret which can only beget an air of reconciliation. Whatever it may be, this is certain—where there is a direct encounter, where there is a *durch-rayden* instead of a *ba-rayden*, where there is a talking the matter over, there is, at the very least, the opportunity of ridding the hostility.

For all these reasons, there is wisdom, as well as morality, in opting for a direct approach. Can I invoke it at this point for selfish considerations? Probably someone won't be in *shul* next Shabbat morning because the rabbi "insulted" him. If he runs true to course, do you know what he is going to do? He's going to tell everyone about it, everyone but me.

There are always members who are angry with the synagogue. Sometimes they are justified in their hurt, sometimes they are not. But even when they're justified, they are wrong. They are wrong because instead of coming to the source and voicing their complaint directly, they go about everywhere beefing and griping, *ba-rayding* and defaming.

It's no great shakes to be a *shaygetz*. Still, short of boorishness, it's a good thing to use the direct approach.

January, 1968

EVERYONE DOES ME SUCH A FAVOR

I am grateful for all the kindnesses that people do me. Without them, I would be stymied before I began. Indeed, the success of much that is my responsibility in the area of adult education programming depends on the good turns that people do me.

By the spring of the year, when we finalize arrangements for the coming season, I manage to work out what I consider to be an eminently impressive and exciting list of guest personalities. And that's when I begin to depend upon people doing me favors.

For one thing, upon our Adult Education Committee and Board. This unquestionably is their business and domain of concern. They want to know more about these academicians that have been proposed and about the relevance of their subject matter for our program and needs. They are especially interested in the pragmatic aspects of my suggestions. How much will it all cost? I am forced to admit that, like everything else in our society today, adult education has become rather expensive. It will, in fact, cost a great deal. They balk when the specifics are revealed. They appreciate the stature of the speakers I would invite and concur that it would be most desirable to hear their views. But can we afford it? Doesn't it mean violating the budget? After all, without denigrating the importance of adult education, there are so many other commitments with which the congregation must reckon.

I understand this kind of response. Their realism is not without merit. But I am persistent in my request. Determined not to lose my cool, I reason, I argue, I sell, I plead. In spite of my resolve, temper gets the best of me. It's a long and arduous and wearing session. In the end, however, it's a rewarding one, and everything turns out all right. In the end, they do the rabbi a favor and go along with his request.

And then there is the favor that the invited lecturers do me. They are, after all, very busy individuals and deeply involved in pursuits of significance. For the most part, getting to Montreal for a particular time means a great deal of inconvenience for them. Is the whole undertaking warranted? How many people will there be in the audience, and what kind of people will they be? Somehow I manage to overcome all their reservations and hesitations. I cajole, I flatter, I convince. Usually I triumph. They'll do me a favor and come.

Above all, I couldn't get by without the great favor that our congregants and local public do me. Were it not for their attendance and participation, then the whole thing would be futile and in vain. I realize that my program must compete with so many other beckoning interests for their time and attention. We live in such a cosmopolitan city, and there is always so much to do. That's why we go all out to summon their patronage. We advertise in the press, we mail special invitations, we have telephone committees. Personally I push it from the pulpit and on every occasion that is open to me. I exhort, I urge, I persuade. And in its way it pays off. Some of them do me a favor and attend.

People do me such favors! *Entre nous,* it isn't the pleasantest of things to be the recipient of favors. That's why, come adult Jewish education, there runs through my mind something that a professor of mine used to say: "Let them die ignorant." Sometimes I feel it's a tempting bit of counsel.

Realistically, however, it's hardly one that any rabbi can afford to accept. He needs, *nebech,* uncomfortable as it may be, to depend on the favors people do him.

October, 1969

FROM ON HIGH

Communications Room,
Hechal-On-High,
Anno Mundi, 5735

Dear Rabbi Cohen:

This is in answer to your prayers, not an answer to your prayers.

And don't be stunned. True, for all My partiality to them, I do not customarily write to rabbis. Somehow, I manage to get through to them short of the mails. If I make an exception now in your instance, it is because I am annoyed, and I want to convey that displeasure in black and white.

This will explain, too, why, while Hebrew is My tongue, English is the medium of the present correspondence. As you have learned in your studies, it is My wont to communicate in the language best understood by My addressees, lest there be any miscomprehension. The holy tongue is My first choice, but English poses no difficulty for Me, and it is important that you get this straight.

I am annoyed—with your prayers. Not the conventional ones which you recite in the *siddur* and at the worship services. Those are fine enough and quite acceptable; although there, too, I wish you, and the others, would be less perfunctory and would mouth them with greater intent and conviction. But the want of *kavanah* is not what piques Me at the moment.

When I aver that I am annoyed with your prayers, I mean your private and unvocalized petitions. You know, from time to time those silent prayers in your heart which, though you are diffident to utter, nevertheless come through to Me loud and clear.

Like your weather prayers, for example. In the warmer seasons, asking for rain on Saturday so that your congregants might make their way to *shul* instead of to the golf courses. And in the winter,

35

with the same pious motivation, quietly praying for no snow lest the ski slopes entice your people away.

Or like your unvoiced prayers for a sniff of anti-Semitism. Noth-for a depression, anything that will cause real suffering; but just for a little bit of recession, so that, how did you put it, affluence shouldn't spoil your people rotten. Just enough of a dip, you suggest, to curb their inflated extravagance and restore their sense of values.

Or like your unvoiced prayers for a sniff of anti-semitism. Nothing serious, you said in your heart, but just enough to scare Jews back to thinking about Me and Israel and their Jewishness. You're all for integration, but you're afraid that they might become too comfortable and forget that they are still in *galut*.

How offensive—your cynicism! It is unworthy of your position as a rabbi to harbor so little faith in your fellow Jews. As if the delights of recreation or the ease of wealth or the freedom of the open society could sway Jews from their Jewishness! For shame, rabbi! You ought to be more circumspect in your prayers—those prayers you hesitate to put into words, but which, nonetheless, My radar picks up in your heart.

I understand that the Canadian Postal Service is not all that efficient. I trust, however, that this letter, in spite of the distance it has to travel, will reach you sooner than later.

Holy yours,
G. Al Mighty

November, 1974

RABBIS ON STRIKE

The rabbis are planning a strike!

Perhaps I'm telling tales out of class, and, doubtlessly, my colleagues won't like this. But I think our *baale-batim* ought to know what's brewing. It's not at all a pleasant prospect. I'm not sure that I favor the idea myself. We've been plagued by altogether too many work stoppages of late, and, frankly, life is becoming intolerable for the innocent public. Still, I'm bound to go along with the majority decision.

When the suggestion was first broached at our meeting, we ourselves could hardly believe our ears. To everyone's knowledge, there was no precedent for it. It would be a first in history. Tinged, however, by the revolutionary spirit of the times, we soon overcame the block of our inherent occupational conservatism. Toying with the idea more seriously now, we focused on the pragmatics of the proposal. Rabbis going out on a strike? Who, queried one of the colleagues, would know?

That line of cynicism, however, was laid to rest as we began to ponder the implications and consequences of such a step.

Religious services in the synagogue might not, perhaps, be that much affected. There are enough laymen who are frustrated rabbis who would be only too eager to replace us there. The academics and teachers in the community would scab in the area of adult Jewish education. But what of our more important functions in the *shul?* What would happen, for example, to the Bar-Mitzvah party, either after the Services or at night, or, for that matter, even in the hotel? A rabbi-less *hamotzi*—say it could be done—just wouldn't be the same and would put a pall on the whole affair. Who would bring the "greetings" and say, as only the rabbi can, all those nice things that are indispensable at such a function? The *simchah* wouldn't be a *simchah*.

37

Weddings would have to be postponed. That might not stop the kids, but it wouldn't sit well with the parents. Moreover, consider the losses that would be incurred by caterers and photographers and florists and printers and couturiers and hairdressers and travel agents—indeed, a whole industry would be shaken. And on the other end of the life cycle, *rachmana litzlan,* people wouldn't stop dying, but what decent person would enjoy being buried without benefit of a rabbinic eulogy?

Patients in the hospitals would be victimized by the stoppage of clergy and chaplaincy visitation, which might very well, God forfend, prolong their convalescence. True, the psychiatrists and family counsellors would reap an advantage from the situation and have a heyday, but think what those unexpected fees would do to the consumer's budget. The price of having problems and being troubled would become unspeakably inflated.

And it would work havoc, too, on an organizational and communal level. With no invocators available to open proceedings, meetings and conferences and conventions would be stymied and aborted even before they began. Besides, one shudders just to imagine how ruinous it would be to our public image. What will the goyim think, what will the non-Jews say about us?

If the rabbis strike, who would know? Don't kid yourself. They wield a powerful clout, and should they go ahead with it, it would spell disaster.

What do the rabbis want? It's not, *chas vechalilah,* anything so mundane as a matter of wages. It's their working conditions that they insist upon being improved. They are demanding a better Sabbath attendance in *shul.* Specifically, they're asking for a 66% raise in attendance this year. This is a wholly justified request, and, indeed, long overdue. But realistically I can see where such a sudden jump must appear exorbitant and arrogant to our *baale-batim.* Personally, therefore, I am ready to accede to a compromise—a 40% raise this year, and 26% the following year.

I think I can sway my colleagues to accept this compromise. I would strongly urge our laymen to be equally conciliatory and come to a settlement without delay. No one, least of all the clergy, would like to see the calamity of a rabbis' strike.

October, 1975

SHABBOS JEWS

It's an obnoxious notion, the idea that *der Rebbe meg*, that the rabbi enjoys special license.

As if position confers special privilege or excuse from law! Au contraire, if anything, office bears with it the burden of special responsibility and punctiliousness.

Our Sages were wont to remind themselves that their role of leadership required of them extra caution in what they said and greater care for the implications of their behavior. For all the equality between them, it is altogether right and justified that come observance, morality, Jewish learning, more be expected of the rabbi than of the layman. Surely, in matters of communal needs, we have reason to expect our professional communal servants to be more alert and circumspect than the average citizen. The sarcasm and bitterness wherewith Jewish folk mouthed *der Rebbe meg* are not only understandable but merited and entirely in order.

But, if we reject the idea that *der Rebbe meg*, we look askance, too, at the specious notion that leadership is charged with the whole responsibility. Indeed, surveying the scene today in this age of specialization, one gets the uneasy feeling that the operative principle is *the layman meg*. There is no gainsaying the boon that professionalism is to society. We do it a grave injustice, however, when we not only demand of it expertise and direction, but shoulder it with the whole job.

The institution of the *Shabbos-goy* is fast disappearing and perhaps with not too many regrets. What bothers is the emergence of the kind of institution that we might call the *Shabbos-Jew*. Of course, the very least we can expect of a rabbi is that he observe the Sabbath. Yet what a distortion it is to leave it all to him and make of the rabbi our *Shabbos-Jew*. I would sincerely hope that my colleagues are more immersed in Jewish learning than the average Jewish layman. But it is not the function of the rabbi to do it all by himself and excuse the *baale-batim* from every and all responsibility in the area of Jewish knowledge.

I'll wager that, by and large, the school is more qualified to teach children than the average home. After all, that's what the whole pedagogic profession is for. Teachers are specialists, and, as such, it is their task to instruct and train our children. How unrealistic, however, to laden the school with the complete mission and relieve the home of all responsibility. There is something palpably wrong with the notion that *the parent meg.*

I, for one, side with the doctrine of *noblesse oblige.* Those who have more should give more. Wealth carries with it added duties and a call for more than an average measure of nobility and largesse. Yet, how unfair the sentiment that is so prevalent which would leave it all to the rich. When a campaign is abroad, there is something distinctly exploitative about an individual who escapes his obligation with the excuse of *ich meg,* "I'm excused."

It's not true that *der Rebbe meg.* Nor is it true that anyone, whatever his position, *meg.* Such liberty-taking creates a society of privileged irresponsibles.

November, 1965

MY DADDY IS IN THE ARMY

Out of the mouths of babes.

It is a Jewish conviction dating way back to Biblical days that children, speaking in their innocence, often pack a punch. The following composition by a seven-year-old girl in grade two in Givatayim, Israel, which I have translated from its original Hebrew, is surely in this category. It's so personal, and yet it speaks a challenge to all of us, wherever we are.

Little Rakefet Sella calls her piece "Daddy is in The Army."

"It's somewhat sad when *abba* (daddy) is in the army," she writes. "On Shabbat, when all the boys and girls go out for hikes, I have to sit in the house. And at night, when every child is kissed by both *imma* (mummy) and *abba*—I am kissed goodnight only by *imma*. When it's announced on the news that a soldier has been wounded or killed—I get frightened and think of my father.

"Sometimes, *abba* comes home. Then I am very happy. When my younger brother and sister fall asleep, I silently creep out to the porch, sit in daddy's lap, and listen to his beautiful stories and ask questions about what happened to him. Afterwards, I part from him with great sorrow, knowing that I shall awake tomorrow and *abba* will not be home.

"How sad and how happy I am that I have an *abba* in the army. Sad—because he's not home; and happy—because daddy is among those who stand ready to protect our country."

Is there anything today that we adults, especially in our society, miss more than the admiration of children? This gnaws at our innards relentlessly and more than we are willing to admit. We do not have the esteem of our progeny. What does it all boot us, if we can't achieve this much—if our children are not proud of us?

There is no implication here that we are wholly at fault. Filial attitudes are a complex phenomenon and are not the consequence

41

solely of parental influence and upbringing. Indubitably, the wider environment, the currency of new ideas, the sway of peer groups, and the ascendancy of a youth cult are all ingredients in the brew. Notwithstanding these obvious realities, it is a truth, too, that we as parents don't exactly generate admiration. The heroic element is lacking in our fabric. Sacrifice is nowhere palpably evident in our persons. In most instances, our kids can't say of their *abba* that he is in the "army" to defend his "country."

After all, we too have "countries" that need protecting. Perhaps not militarily, but surely through a guise of commitment and dedication that involves sacrifice. We live in multiple "countries." Never before has the country of our Judaism here in the Diaspora, besieged as it is by the annihilating forces of the surrounding open society, been so threatened. For all that it doesn't command our political allegiance and citizenship, beleaguered Israel is still our country. At the very least, we all live in the country of family and marriage. And the weal of this state is rigidly being undermined. No one with open eyes can be unaware of the protection needed for the decency of our civilization and morality of our culture.

The fact is, we are not in the army. Our young people do not see their parents heroically making sacrifices for Jewishness, for Zionism, for familism, for ethics and morality.

October, 1970

NAGGING HAS ITS POINTS

We give up too easily.

This is true in almost every area of our living today. Face to face with an obstacle, confronted by a challenge, somehow we seem to lack the gumption to put up a fight. Is it because we are too tired, or indifferent, or cynical? Patently, missing in us is that *conatus* which is so necessary for the preservation of principle and the achievement of goal.

I see it, this surrender, so frequently in parents. "And if I tell him, will he listen to me?" It is as if we know a priori that there is no laying down the law to our children once they reach a certain age. I'm not sure that laying down the law is what we're really after. But even in instances of counselling and direction, even in instances of conveying our will, we take it for granted that we shall get nowhere. We voice our sentiments, yet beyond that, we don't persist as compellingly as we might. Defeated from the start, we desist from nagging.

Recently, the American Jewish Congress reported some interesting results of a study that had been conducted for it by the Bureau of Applied Social Research of Columbia University on intermarriage and interdating. While it was found that one-third of the Jewish students on a college campus engaged in interreligious dating, the rate amongst the Catholic students was 76 percent and amongst the Protestants 60 percent. Furthermore, two-thirds of the Catholic students involved in the study considered it likely that they would marry outside their faith, against 46 percent of the Protestant students and 15 percent of the Jewish students.

Most significant in the study, however, was the finding that parents had a strong influence on the students' dating behavior and marriage plans. According to the report, in all the three religious groups, students who believed their parents would disapprove of their interdating were less likely to date outside their religion or to consider intermarriage. In this instance, too, the statistics are comparatively more heartening to us. While 76 percent of the Catholic students and 70 percent of the Protestants said that they ignored their parents' objections to interdating, the figure of obstinacy amongst Jewish students was 47 percent. In other words, the study revealed that Jewish students were more likely to be affected by pressures from parents aimed at discouraging interdating and intermarriage.

To be sure, one should be wary about building his case on mere statistics. But there is the indication here that parental pressure, uncomfortable and unpleasant as it may be, is not without its results in the total picture. There is no suggestion here that the whole solution to the grave problem of intermarriage lies wholly in the hands of parents. It is a very complex issue and involves so many different factors. Yet, there is good reason to believe that where parents defy the cynicism of "will he listen to me?", that where parents go out of their way to be in touch with the social life of their children, that where parents are unsophisticated enough to badger and nag, they can in large measure keep their children from interdating and the possible pitfalls that issue therefrom. Parents need more gumption to put up a fight.

November, 1965

TZEDAKAH IS SELF-TAXATION

This is in the way of a protest against the high cost of charity. Let no one misconstrue the nature of the demur. I am not now taking sides with the oft-heard complaint about the increasing demands made upon us for our generosity. The fact is that in an age of affluence it costs more to meet philanthropic needs. It's all part and parcel of the high cost of living in every sphere of our existence. Moreover, our whole concept of help has been broadened and deepened. We're beginning to understand that real aid consists of more than just immediate relief and emergency alleviation. Today we entertain as altogether legitimate, and even prudent, long-range programs of assistance and extended kinds of services.

No, when I balk at the high cost of charity, I'm irritated by something else. I'm annoyed by the excessive expense involved in raising funds for legitimate needs. All too often, these expenditures are out of all proportion to the objective realized, and more often than not, incongruous with the spirit of the cause. Whether it be of a single institution or of a wider communal nature, the contemporary campaign tends to resort to gimmickery; and, in a blasé generation such as ours, in order to make the desired impact, this gimmickery is necessarily high-priced.

To make money, one must spend money. There is merit to this tack, and, indeed, experience confirms it. But are we not overdoing the principle? Jewish tradition counsels circumspection in the use of community means and belabors wastefulness. There is, undoubtedly, something immoral about eliciting from the community sizable sums for gimmickery that could be much better used in other directions. There is something palpably wrong, for example, when a net of ten thousand dollars for a worthwhile project costs a congregation five thousand dollars.

With whom does the blame lie? With the campaigners, who operate with a "Madison Avenue" mentality? One does get the impression that there is much too much easy resort to sensationalism and dramatics. On the other hand, there is no denying the indifference and imperviousness of the modern public. At the root of it all is the lack of a genuine motivation of *tzedakah*. We can be entertained into giving, banqueted and feted into giving; but it's much harder to get us to give simply out of a sense of our obligation to a deserving cause. That is, is it not, the real meaning of *tzedakah* —a kind of self-taxation, a feeling of responsibility to the needs round about us.

In the dissipation of Jewish values, which is the mark of our times, one gets the uneasy feeling that, for all our vaunted virtue of philanthropy, our attribute of *tzedakah* is also evaporating. For were it sincerely with us, this quality of *tzedakah*, the cost of our charity would not be so high. Or to put it another way, were we really the philanthropic folk we like to believe ourselves to be, we could get a lot more out of what we give.

January, 1966

UNFULFILLED POTENTIAL

Freedom is living up to one's potential.

To be sure, we have, in our contemporary spirit of permissiveness, transmuted the ideal of enjoying liberty into the ugliness of taking liberties. Freedom is certainly one of our chiefest blessings, but there is no gainsaying our abuse of it when we go too far. On the other hand, there is the reverse side of the coin. If we abuse it when we go too far, we vitiate it no less when we don't go far enough. Freedom is living up to your potential.

In this light, I wonder whether we really enjoy the freedom to believe, whether we live up to our potential of faith.

I am persuaded that inherent in every individual is a spiritual dimension, a fundamental religious *weltanschauung* that begs for fulfillment. Rob man of his theological mooring, and he will grasp for surrogates. This explains, in measure, I suppose, the efflorescence of astrology and exotic cults *davka* in our scientific and sophisticated times. In his arresting study, *Identity—Youth and Crisis,* Erik Erikson speaks of the "sense of wholeness," of the "wholeness of existence," wherewith religious faith informs man.

I am not now speaking of faith in any creedal sense. Rather does that term mean for me a reasoned-out thesis whose construct of things affords us, intellectually and emotionally, an integrating philosophy of life, a premise and outlook which provide us with direction in our existence and root us in a system of values. Willy-nilly, at some time or other, we are all bothered by what we refer to as the great and basic questions of life. What's it all about? Desultory and casual ruminations in this realm, however, hardly suffice. The tragedy is that we don't make a more exhaustive effort to think things through profoundly. We do not live up to our theological potential. For all our liberty, we are not free to believe.

Some years ago, a rabbi from Boston met a colleague from Phila-

47

delphia and had occasion to complain that, inasmuch as Boston was the center of Unitarianism, many Jews were parading as Unitarians. "It's not much better in Philadelphia," commiserated his colleague. "Philadelphia, as you know, is the seat of Quakerism, and some of our best Jews are Friends."

That's not our Achilles heel nowadays. Today Jews don't consciously withdraw from Jewish life to pass for what they are not. There is little deliberate assimilation. But the fact remains that what passes for Jewish life is so woefully watery and indistinctively Jewish. We don't use a Jewish tongue. Most of us don't celebrate Jewish events. We don't bear Jewish names. Our values and morality hardly shine any longer for their Jewish distinctiveness. We are, in this respect, as pagan as the heathen culture round about us.

All this bespeaks no designed pursuit of assimilation. It does, however, abundantly semaphore our arrant failure to live up to our potential to create in this milieu, where we are at liberty to do so, and with a measure of means and wealth and know-how that no other Jewish community has ever had in history, a visible, vibrant, vigorous Jewish life. I am not asking for the moon and stars. I know we cannot duplicate here the density of Jewishness that obtains in Israel. But surely ours is the opportunity and the ability to flesh out what is now no more than a skeletal Judaism. We shall only experience the freedom to be Jews when we live up to our Jewish potentialities.

March, 1971

KNOW THE PLACE

Ayeh hamakom?

If there is any phrase in the Hebrew language which the poorest of Hebrew School students will remember long after he has forgotten almost everything else, it is that query which teachers diabolically employed to make sure that you were paying attention and following the lesson in the text—*ayeh hamakom?* I can still hear it ringing in my ears from my own student days. I can still hear myself reiterating it when I was a teacher in the classroom. I heard it just the other day when I visited a grade in our school —*ayeh hamakom?* Where is the place?

Where is the place? If our contemporary Jewish life is on the wan and pale side and palpably is not as healthy and vibrant as it should be, it strikes me that in great measure it can be attributed to the fact that we don't know where the place is. I mean, too many of us don't know *vu men halt*, where things are at. I'm not sure that I know what the reason is; there is probably a variety of explicative factors, such as indolence, or indifference, or perhaps an over-preoccupation with other interests. Whatever the reason, quite patently too many of us are not paying attention; with the result that we don't know the place, we're not aware of and in touch with what is going on in Jewish life. If I may borrow a phrase from my son's lingo, we're not with it.

It struck me with no little sadness last year when it was announced that Samuel Joseph Agnon, the Hebrew novelist, was awarded the Nobel Prize for literature. Truthfully, how many of us had ever heard of Agnon, let alone how many had ever read him? That the average Canadian should not know of him is altogether understandable. But that the average American or Canadian Jew should be totally ignorant of this great Jewish writer of our times is, no matter how you rationalize it, a depressing fact.

49

This nescience illustrates only too vividly and too conclusively that the vast majority of our Jews here are totally unaware of that great and exciting development in the annals of our people—the renascence of the Hebrew culture and civilization that is transpiring in our age. Indubitably, it's a development which is destined to be a watershed in Jewish history, yet the lugubrious fact is that we are not with it.

At the recent World Conference of Ashkenazi and Sephardi Synagogues, the President of the Union of Orthodox Jewish Congregations of U.S. and Canada, according to press releases, attacked Reform and Conservative Judaism and asserted that there was no place for these divisive ideologies in Israel. It makes for painful reading—the periodic news of these extremist Jews here and in Israel who would exclude every form of non-orthodox religious Judaism in the Jewish State. This ugly exhibition of unabated and even venomous intolerance calls to mind Santayana's wonderful definition of fanaticism. Fanaticism, he said, is redoubling your effort when you have forgotten your aim. Surely it is patent that Jews who, in this day and age and in this period of ecumenism, advocate the suppression of religious freedom simply don't know *vu men halt.*

This is a vastly different world from that of the pre-Emancipation era and the *shtetl.* What makes the primary and crucial difference is that totally new phenomenon—the advent of secular democracy. It is simply an inveterate datum of our system that we are at liberty today to profess and practice as much or as little religion as we desire. Anyone who is with it must appreciate that diversity in this area is part and parcel of the scene and must be respected. Jewish unity today cannot be envisaged in terms of uniformity, but only in terms of community, or to use Mordecai Kaplan's phrase, "unity in diversity." People who champion the idea of a monolithic Judaism simply don't know where the place is in the history book.

Ayeh hamakom? Whatever else is worthwhile knowing, it's well at all times to know the answer to this question, or shall we say, to this challenge.

February, 1968

KNOW YOUR PLACE

Where is *your* place?

In our last piece we were perturbed by the fact that some people "don't know the place," don't know *vu men halt*—are not in tune with the spirit and significance of the hour. But suppose you do know the place; we are propelled to delve a bit deeper and ask: where is *your* place?

What we are lamenting in this piece is that all too often we don't know our place. Let no one take umbrage; there is no espousal here of any kind of servility. We are merely stating a truth—very frequently in our Jewish life, as in so many other ambits of our existence, we are led to make decisions and pass judgments in areas where we have no competence. Individuals who possess no intellectual and cultural Jewish background, because of their leadership positions, determine the status and destiny of Jewish education in the community. People who religiously are simply unequipped rule and govern religious institutions and set religious policy. Parents who pedagogically and subject-wise are uninformed feel themselves altogether free to interfere with the professional administration and help run the school.

I appreciate that behind this whole phenomenon there is a pulsating spirit of democracy and egalitarianism. I have every respect for the democratic process in our society, every regard for the principle of equality. Yet, with all due deference to "our rights," good sense dictates that I ought to know my place—that, for all my privilege and liberty to do so, there are instances where, in view of my inadequacy, I should be more hesistant to throw my weight around.

To know your place. It means the converse too. There are times when precisely because of your adequacy and backround and equipment, you should meddle and have a say.

I was speaking to a real intellectual the other day, a man with

51

an unusually fine Jewish and secular background. He lives in a populous Jewish community on the outskirts of New York City. I asked him if he was involved in the administration of his synagogue, whether, for example, he was a member of its school committee—for I knew full well that congregation would very much prize the services of such an individual. He said that he took no part in such activities, that he didn't have the temperament for that sort of thing. Isn't that precisely one of the weaknesses of contemporary Jewish life, that temperament and not competence produces our leadership?

Someone remarked recently that "buck-passing is not new—but they never passed faster than they do now." I suggest that, while the joke in the statement is an allusion to our inflation, the original meaning of the phrase buck-passing, shifting the responsibility, is a universal and pervasive phenomenon of our time. The fact is, in Jewish life, as in all areas that call for voluntary participation, capable people irresponsibly refuse to carry their load and fill the positions which are rightfully theirs to fill. They don't know, because they don't want to know, their place.

We all have our particular place in the text of history. It's important to know where your place is.

February, 1968

MAKE PLACE

To be frank about it, the answer lies in *making* place.

Somehow in these last few pieces we've gotten hung up on the notion of "place". We felt that if Jewish life here is not as vibrant and healthy as it should be, the reason hinges very largely on this matter of place. For one thing, too many of us are not in step with the place we have reached on the modern scene. Again, we tend for one reason or another to play truant and absent ourselves from the place that is rightfully ours in the context of Jewish life. Can I now round off this excursion into a trilogy by asking: what place do we *make* in our scheme of things for our Jewishness?

I appreciate the fact that we are all of us busy individuals, with heavy commitments, responsibilities, and varied interests. I am aware that you are not like a rabbi, who works only on Shabbat and then has very little to do the rest of the week—and when he is busy, is, to boot, by the very nature of his calling, occupied with things Jewish. I know that generally speaking there isn't too much room in your schedule for the expansive kind of Jewish life that is ideally advocated. So what's the answer? That you're going to get your Jewishness in bits and pieces, in dribs and drabs, whenever you have an odd moment or two? In practice, I'm afraid that is precisely the solution. For most of us, ours is a desultory Jewishness, it's a Jewishness of snatches.

Down deep everyone appreciates that this kind of hit and miss Judaism is in no wise a rewarding experience. Obviously what is called for, if our identity is to be meaningful at all, is a restructuring of our schedule, a basic change in the very pattern of our life. In our busy scheme of things, we have to shift our priorities and make room and place for a regularity of Jewish experiences.

They tell of Alfred Smith that, when he was Governor of New York, he received a letter inquiring if he had ever read Horatio

53

Alger books. A single sentence reply came from his secretary: "Governor Smith asks me to tell you that he never read any books, and Alger's was among them." I don't know—perhaps it's because you don't read any books, and Jewish books are among them. Perhaps it's because at your age you don't study anything, and Jewish study is included. Perhaps it's because you are not a mixer and you steer clear of all associations and entanglements, and Jewish organizations are no exception. I don't know your habits and traits, but, whatever they are, at the moment they are irrelevant. The whole point is we are talking now about creating new habits and traits, about making room in our personal round of existence for Jewish practices and indulgences.

A young lad announced to his mother that he was going out into the yard to play ball with God. "How do you play ball with God?" asked the puzzled mother. "It's easy," explained the boy. "I just throw the ball up in the air and God throws it back down to me." Well, to play ball with God—I don't know if it's that easy. But surely it isn't too hard. Essentially all it calls for is, on a regular basis, setting aside a little time each week to pray and worship, to read a passage in His Book. It's a felicitous phrase—"to play ball with," it has the connotation of being fair with. Are we really playing ball with God, are we really being fair with our religious heritage when we settle for odd snatches, instead of making an ample and regular place for it in our schedule of things?

February, 1968

A JEW IS IN A NAME

I don't necessarily endorse it, but I'm not upset by it—changing our surnames.

What does perturb me is the nature of the given names we select for our children. By and large, we look askance at altering our Jewish-sounding family names. On the other hand, we think nothing of affixing our off-spring with names that haven't the remotest connection with Hebrew and Jewish character. It's an interesting switch! Vis-à-vis the non-Jewish world we want to identify ourselves unmistakably as Jews. But *entre nous*, between our children and ourselves in the home, we are satisfied with appelations that evoke no ambience of Jewishness. In one sense, I suppose, that's quite commendable. We insist that the non-Jewish world know us for the Jews we are. In another sense, however, it borders on the shameful. Amongst ourselves we are much less heedful of our Jewish being.

True enough, we give our children Jewish names. The fact is, however, these cognomens are scarcely ever used. Already in registering children in kindergarten, we encounter difficulty in determining the Jewish name selected only five years earlier. In writing the *ketubah* at marriage time, increasingly we find that not only the young couple but even their parents are at a loss to remember the Jewish names. For all intents and purposes, Jewish names today are a one-time happening. Ceremoniously invoked at birth, they are not again used.

For myself, I'd sooner see Hurwitz become Haines but remain Mordecai, than for Hurwitz to be retained and Mordecai become Malcolm.

And I don't feel that I am making a mountain out of a molehill. What's in a name? In one respect, very little. In another respect, however, a great deal—especially in a name which is employed by people who are near and close and dear to you. The important area of our living is where we go by our first names. This is where the relationships count most.

"As is his name, so he is," remarks Scripture. The Sages in the Talmud speak of the influential role which a name plays in a person's life. We know it from our own experience. Epithets stir feelings and create moods. Isn't that the explanation of pet names and sobriquets of endearment? What's in a name? Everything! There's association in a name! There's expectation! There's a *shtimmung!* There's identification!

It does something subtle and intangible, but profound and decisive, both to the child and to the parent when there is a Jewish ring to the appellation. It makes a heap of difference in a household when the name heard is Gershon rather than Gregory; makes a heap of difference to a young lad when he grows up as Hillel rather than as Hilary.

I'm all for introducing the vogue of giving our children Hebraic-sounding names. In many a home, such an invocation would be the only remainder of a Jewish tongue, the only constant exemplification of *Yiddishkeit.* In every setting such a name cannot but create a Jewish atmosphere that otherwise would be lacking.

It is far more important that we sound Jewish *entre nous* than *entre les autres!*

May, 1968

PAST GLORIES AREN'T ENOUGH

What about now?

My sixteen-year-old son spent the better part of this past summer in Israel as a participant in the Ramah Israel Seminar. It was for him a very memorable and maturing experience.

In spite of the mail strike, we managed to hear rather frequently from Raphael and shared vicariously in his charged discovery of Israel and its people. Forgive this paternal indulgence, but I am propelled now to cite a few lines from one of his letters. "I don't know how this affected my *kehunah*, but I decided that it was my duty as a Jew to visit the military cemetery where I could see the tombs of 18-year-olds from the War of Liberation, the Sinai Campaign, and the Six Day War. We then went on to the Hadassah Hospital—the new one—where we had a tour. We saw a helicopter landing soldiers wounded in an incident of that day with Jordan in which a major was killed. Once inside the hospital I experienced my most moving moment in Israel. An unconscious and bloodied soldier was being rolled in on a stretcher. To me the idea of knowing that there lay a Jewish soldier who had fought to defend Israel, being cared for in a Hebrew hospital by Hebrew doctors and nurses, was more real and more stirring than the Western Wall or Tomb of David, or the Tomb of Rachel. To me this was Israel in its beautiful or not so beautiful reality."

It's not that the Western Wall and the Tomb of the Patriarchs do not fire the emotions; it's not that the evidence of the past is unimportant or irrelevant. Obviously, one is awed by the visible remnants of yesteryears' greatness. Everyone stands in reverence before history. When, however, you speak in terms of being stirred, when it's a matter of being captivated, then you need the reality of present greatness and living example. Leastwise, this is the way it goes with our young people. To elicit their excitement and devotion it takes more than a museum—it takes reality.

57

Is there perchance here something of an explication of the luke-warmness that characterizes the attitude of our youth to their Jewishness in our part of the world? They are far from being defectors, and it would be an injustice to regard them as escapists. Our young people are not engaged in any conscious programs of assimilation. They are, however, too many of them, drifting away through indifference and apathy. Patently there is nothing in the milieu of Jewish life which we offer them that excites their admiration and commands their commitment.

Young people need the inspiration of a present reality. At best they see in our part of the world a celebration of Judaism's past glories. Lamentably, they are not witness to contemporary Jewish greatness. We offer them scarce and scant example of nobility, the reality of Jews who make sacrifices for Jewish living. Very bluntly, there is very little in our mode of life that is Jewishly inspiring and challenging.

Thank God for the example of Israel. But we need here, too, the demonstration of daily sacrifice for Jewish life.

August, 1968

JEWISH EDUCATION—CAUSE OR EFFECT?

I wonder if we're not putting the cart before the horse.

Some weeks ago, under the aegis of the Canadian Jewish Congress, a conference of leaders was held in our community to deal with a very grave problem. Statistics have revealed that eleven thousand nine hundred and sixty Jewish children of elementary and secondary school age in our city and its environs are receiving no Jewish education whatsoever. When we are minded that the school population of Jewish children is some nineteen thousand strong, the arithmetic is clear—more than one half of our youth is getting no Jewish education. Even allowing for inaccuracy and exaggeration in the count, the datum remains dismaying and shattering. Jewish education is the lifeblood of our existence, and we are growing palpably anemic.

Understandably, the conference assigned top priority to the task of recruiting greater numbers of our children for Jewish tuition. In the course of the lively and earnest discussion, a variety of ideas and suggestions were distilled. The strategies, on the whole, were cogent and promisingly valid. They are certainly worth a try. If implemented, they might well yield some positive results.

Some results, but scarcely more. For the feeling grew on me, as I sat there listening to the colloquy, that we were not getting down to the root of the matter. The general premise was that Jewish education is the instrument par excellence for the generation and preservation of our Jewishness. And that, it struck me, is where we were putting the cart before the horse. I'm convinced that it's the other way around. I am persuaded that, fundamentally, it is our Jewishness which motivates Jewish education, and not vice versa. Surely a proper reading of our history will confirm that the intensity of Jewish learning, for example, in the European communities of yore, was the effect, and not the cause, of the vibrant Jewishness of that clime.

59

One can adduce any number of reasons to explain the diminution of Jewish education in our milieu. I shall not deny that the strictures are, in some measure, warrantable and legitimate. But to peg the real blame on economics, on irrelevancy or incompetent teaching—that ilk of explication—is nothing short of fatuous. Parents aren't providing their children with Jewish schooling primarily because they are not Jewishly motivated. They aren't interested in Jewishness, hence they aren't concerned about Jewish education.

From my own vantage, Jewishness here in the Golah is necessarily and essentially of a religious dimension. Thus, it is no accident that a strong correlation exists between religious traditionalism on the one hand, and Jewish education on the other. And no accident either that a correlation obtains between the growth of Jewish secularity on the one hand, and, in spite of Israel's being on the scene, the growth in the numbers of our young people who are Jewishly nescient and untutored on the other hand. Jewish nationalism is not yet tantamount to Jewishness. Interpret it as you will, the latter is still substantially synonymous with *Yiddishkeit*.

And so I'm constrained to conclude that, save we become more concerned about our Judaism before we get hung up on Jewish education per se, we shall be putting the cart before the horse.

February, 1971

BEGIN WITH THE RAISON D'ÊTRE

What came first, the chicken or the egg?

That, ever so many people have chided me, is the conundrum into which I worked myself in the previous article. I was grappling with the distressing problem of the decline of Jewish education in our communities and came to a rather heretical conclusion. It seemed to me that we were going at it in a cart-before-the horse fashion. It's not so much the case of Jewish education creating Jewishness, as it is Jewishness which creates Jewish education. In other words, what ails us is not the lack of Jewish education, but rather the lack of Jewish motivation. Given the latter, the will to be Jewish, and the former, Jewish education, will necessarily be revivified.

And that's where I backed myself into the conundrum. Granted, rabbi, you are right; but how do you generate a will for Judaism save through Jewish education? What came first, the chicken or the egg?

I am sensitive to the enigma. And let no one misread me into imagining that I am ready to dispense with Jewish education. Of course, *ha beha talya*, there is an inexorable interdependence between Judaism and learning. Conceding the interplay between the two, however, must not deter us from ascribing priority to the one over the other. Personally, I am of the strong persuasion that the chicken came before the egg.

You start with Judaism.

You begin with the idea—the premise, the faith, the conviction —that since time immemorial the Jew has been called into being for a very special role, for the purpose of exemplifying on earth the divine way of life. If you don't fancy the term "mission," put it this way—as a Jew you have a particular "vocation" in the history of mankind.

61

Commencing with this proposition, you take a second step. Going beyond a mere intellectual stance, you commit yourself to that idea, and thus translate it into an ideology. You submit to an undertaking. You stand in readiness, through any and all courses which may be necessary, to enact your conviction and bear testimony to it. You agree to live your idea.

And there is need, abundant need, for you to be the Jew and persevere in your vocation. For all the dazzle and sophistication of our civilization, it remains far removed from that type of world which can be honestly characterized as divine. The Jew's job is not yet done, and Judaism has still to fulfill its goal. As a Jew, you have an unparallelled and unique contribution to make to the society of man.

This smacks of arrogance? Perhaps. But, from a different angle, it's more an instance of stalwart responsibility than vain presumptuousness. Tradition would inform us with the need of being partners with God in the continuous shaping of our world.

This is not education as such. This is a bold conviction. Given this motivation—let the Jewish community be seized with a sense of call and responsibility, with an awareness of the raison d'être of Judaism—and all else will follow. Let Jews be propelled by a drive of purpose, and they will betake themselves to Torah and learning to find the wherewithal of its effectuation. Jewish will and commitment beget Jewish education.

When our forefathers at Sinai, in their response to the divine invitation which inaugurated the Jewish adventure, antefixed "we shall do" to "and we shall learn," were they not of the mind that the chicken comes before the egg?

March 5, 1971

JEWISH GOYIM

The *goyim* find it hard to understand us.

There are any number of facets of our Jewishness that are passing strange in the sight of non-Jews. But what nonplusses them the most is the inextricable nexus that exists between our religion and peoplehood. In the Christian universe of discourse, faith and nationalism are disparate phenomena and things apart. Indeed, in the story of Christianity, religion transcends ethnic delimitations and is intolerant of national particularism.

Given the Christian orientation, then, it is difficult to comprehend our insistence upon interlocking our religion with Jewish nationalism. This goes a far way in explaining why even the *tov shebagoyim*, the friendliest and best of the non-Jews, can with equanimity oppose the State of Israel and not feel themselves anti-Semitic. They simply cannot fathom the fact that, unlike Christianity, Judaism is not just a religion, but that it is rather the religion of a particular people. This is what, somehow, we must convey to them, especially in these days which are so critical for the State of Israel—that, unlike Christianity, which has only the Church, Judaism has not only the Synagogue, but the Land too.

If there are *goyim* who are confused by the relationship in Judaism between Synagogue and Land, there are Jewish *goyim* who are confounded by the relationship in Judaism between Land and Synagogue.

Jewish *goyim*. I do not use the phrase derisively or pejoratively. I mean it literally—our own people for whom being Jewish is only a matter of being a *goy*, a nation, like all the other nations, and nothing more. We have our own people who would, in their own way, violate the uniqueness of the Jewish entity by deracinating its religious dimensions.

We are witness to this evisceration when, from time to time, at-

63

tempts are made to define the Jew in wholly and exclusively secular terms. We insist that in Judaism there is Land. We insist no less that in Judaism there is also the Synagogue. Golda Meir expressed it most pungently when, in defending the Amendment to the Law of Return which retained the essential religious definition of the Jew, she said:

"I am not religiously observant, but had it not been for religion, we would have shared the fate of all those peoples who have disappeared. We are fortunate indeed that there are still synagogues in Moscow, Odessa and Leningrad serving as the only center for Jews to which they come, at least on Simhat Torah, as an outlet for their feelings of Jewish identity. I would like to tell you that in 1948 when I attended synagogue on Rosh Hashanah and Yom Kippur in Moscow, I did not stir from my place the whole day. I thought to myself that had I stayed longer at that post I would have gone to synagogue not out of duty as the representative of the Jewish State, but because I, Golda Meir, my place is in the synagogue along with other Jews. Above all else, in my views and that of the overwhelming majority of the members of the Knesset, the survival of Israel comes first, before the State of Israel, before Zionism. . . . Any price is worth paying for the security of the State of Israel, as long as it is realized that its role is to preserve the Jewish people. Otherwise it is pointless. This measure may not succeed in reducing the incidence of inter-marriage but at least it will grant no *heter* for it."

A Jew is a complex being who, at the very least, reckons both with the Land and the Synagogue.

April, 1971

SECULAR DEFINITIONS WON'T DO

What is, at one and the same time, both smaller and bigger than the State of Israel?

Jewish nationality.

Smaller. That's obvious from the fact that, while the majority of people living in Israel are Jews, and while it is unmistakably a Jewish state, the citizenry of Israel is a broader entity, including as it does individuals who are not of the Jewish nation. That's the point of nationality on the Israeli identity card. An Arab in Beersheba is an Israeli citizen, but that hardly makes him a member of the Jewish nation. Druze and Christian subjects of the Jewish state are by no stretch of the imagination Jewish. It is the dominant one in Israel; Jewish nationality, however, is only one of a variety of nationalities extant in that state. In Israel, Jewish nationality is smaller than Jewish statehood.

And yet it is bigger, far bigger, too. No one will contend, not even the most rabidly chauvinistic Israeli, that Israel incorporates the entire Jewish nation. More Jews live outside its boundaries than within its borders. Nor is this just a matter of the physical distribution of the Jews. As a consequence of historical forces and developments, Jewish peoplehood has come to transcend geography as such. Without in any way denigrating the central significance of Israel for us, still the fact of the matter is that the phenomenon of Jewish nationhood—philosophically, historically, and pragmatically—is bigger than Jewish statehood.

All of which makes the recent decision of Israel's Supreme Court on the question of Who Is A Jew distinctly unfortunate. I appreciate that the justices were, from their point of view, ruling on an exclusively Israeli matter—who, under Israeli law, was to be regarded as a Jew by nationality. For all intents and purposes, however, their decision, had it been allowed to remain, would have had

65

profound and critical ramifications for the Jewish world at large. One wants to guard against oversimplification. There is no gainsaying the problem which confronted the Israeli authorities—how does one, in a modern and secular state, determine, for purposes of law and registration, who is a Jew? I personally am not inclined to theocratic exercises in the affairs of state. This time, however, the issue exceeded religion and politics.

The Israeli Supreme Court was seized with an issue which *volens-nolens* had to affect the Jewish people everywhere. As such, it would seem to me that the better part of wisdom would have dictated a refusal to tamper with a matter that is bigger and beyond the scope of the Jewish state—the nature of Jewish nationality. Secular definitions of who is a Jew may come quite simply and without too much consequence in a Jewish state. But where is the concern for what such a tack would do to Jewish nationhood and Jewish life in the Galut? Reducing Jewish nationality to a sheer secular phenomenon would indubitably open the floodgates of intermarriage here and pull the rug from under the feet of our survival as a people in the Diaspora.

Separate nationality and religion. Good, I can conceive of a man being an atheist and still being a Jew. But for the life of me, I can't conceive, even in Israel, of a Catholic priest being a Jew. Who is a Jew? At the very least, one who is not of a non-Jewish faith. Somehow, at root, there is some kind of a connection between Jewishness and Judaism that no secularism, no matter how logical and thoroughgoing, can erase.

February, 1970

AN INERADICABLE JEWISHNESS

The holiness of Old Jerusalem and The Wall.

Strange, in a way, even for the securalist Jew in Israel and abroad. That these sites should awaken a sense of sanctity in the religious among us is altogether understandable. That it should do almost no less in the non-religious among us is at once somewhat perplexing and revealing.

Soldiers' Talk very effectively captures the sentiments and reactions of the Israeli fighters immediately after the Six Day War. In this remarkable chronicle of conversations with kibbutzniks who had just returned from the army, Lotan says: "In spite of the fact that I am not religious, the City very much spoke to me, the Wall spoke to me . . . I felt that the Wall is not only a wall, it's not only stones but rather it's an expression." In a similar vein, Uzzi remarks: "I personally say as soon as you hear 'Jerusalem,' you have a different feeling . . . I have no connection whatsoever with the religious—no one can suspect me of that—but this is something that touches all of us. More than anything else it gets you."

From our vantage, it is somewhat amusing. Our securalist friends in Israel now speak of the *beayah,* the problem, that Jerusalem is to them—the problem of explaining the fact that, though they are not religious, Old Jerusalem and the Western Wall presented a special experience for them. Actually, of course, it is essentially a religious experience. They, however, are afraid to admit as much. They use circumlocution. Of their reaction to seeing the Wall for the first time they say, "There was something in it."

What was that something? Just history, and no more? About to enter upon the battle for Jerusalem, one soldier allows, "Tonight we enter upon history." "Opposite the history of the Jewish people," says another soldier of his standing in front of the Wall.

But it was more than just history. Hebron, too, was history; Shechem, too, was history. Why this special feeling for Jerusalem and the Wall?

Shai tells it this way: "When I heard in my unit, on the transistor, about the conquest of Jerusalem, there wasn't one who didn't cry, me included. Then I felt for the first time *lo et hayisraeliut*, not the Israeliness, *ela et hayehudiut*, but rather the Jewishness, of the people." How revealing! Somehow Jerusalem was bigger than the Land and the State. Somehow there was a mystique to Jerusalem which infused a sense of Jewishness.

Perhaps it's best dramatized in an episode related by Tziviah. "We were in the hospital, and they announced over the radio 'Jerusalem has been taken.' Then, at the moment they said that Jerusalem was won, instinctively, all the soldiers lying in bed and holding transitors put something on their heads—one a newspaper, another a handkerchief, another a shirt." Rachel is sceptical and interrupts unbelievingly: "Non-religious soldiers?!" And Tziviah continues: "All of them . . . all the attendants. Even the girls put something on their heads."

Indubitably, it's as one religious soldier put it when he saw comrades, who ostensibly were bereft of any feeling of holiness, excited at the Wall: "Then I understood again that which I imagined before, that there is in us, in the whole Jewish people—in the secularists as well as in the religious—a deep Jewish quality that can never be eradicated."

May, 1970

A HEALTHY PLACE IN THE WELFARE STATE

A new challenge for Jewish life here is in the making.

It's the Welfare State. Everywhere on this continent developments are in that direction. Here in Quebec, for good and sundry
reasons, its emergence is more palpable and rapid. Speaking in
our midst the other day, a respected news analyst allowed that
within five to ten years a full-blown Welfare State would be upon us.

It makes little difference whether or not we favor its coming.
Personally, I am persuaded that social justice is the better served by
this evolution. But regardless of one's likes or dislikes, and irrespective of one's politics, some form of a Welfare State is a modern
inevitability. All deference to individualism. Given our stage of
technological progress and social awareness, however, we are necessarily in for a much larger dosage of collectivity and governmental
control.

The spectre of this eventuality is creating a feeling of unease in
Jewish circles. And rightfully so, for it is attended by especial
implications for Jewish life that are no little perturbing. There
is no playing here at prescience. Only a fool would dare to predict
what is going to be. At the same time, a reasoned concern for, and
a rational anticipation of what is potentially in the making, are in
order and the dictate of prudence.

The Welfare State is going to change radically the character of
our Jewish community. The auspices of a number of important
institutions and agencies will no longer be specifically ours. Even
allowing for a vestigial kind of religious pattern and ethnicity,
such important areas as governance, administration, policy-making,
and philosophy will become the prerogative and responsibility of
non-sectarian officialdom. The tremendous Jewish effort and activ-
ity that are elicited by our existing Jewish institutions, both on the
part of professionals and lay volunteers, will become largely super-

fluous and will evaporate. Even our customary philanthropy bids well to be adversely affected. The sentiment will be abroad that governmental support and maintenance obviate the need for our heretofore wonted generosity.

There is no gainsaying that for many Jews, perhaps even for the majority in our milieu, the prime and sole expression and experience of Jewishness lie in their identification with and participation in Jewish communitiness, in their interest in and preoccupation with the more visible and corporate manifestations of Jewish peoplehood. And the whole point now is that, given the Welfare State, there will be less of this conventional kind of communitiness around to summon their loyalty. Much of what now comprises our Jewish communitiness—the Jewish hospitals and health services, the Jewish welfare agencies and social service, the specialized Jewish facilities for the exceptional young and the aged, and all their attendant organizations and enterprises—will be attenuated. In the Welfare State, the average modern Jewish secuarlist will find meagre fare to satisfy and express his sense of Jewishness. Thus will our open society afford him yet another impetus to dissolve in the melting pot and assimiliate.

But all this need not be. A new and genuine emphasis upon the spiritual and cultural essence of Jewishness, a seizure with the positive stuff of Judaism, can resuscitate in us the real purposiveness of Jewish living and give us a sound and healthy place in the Welfare State. We need a new constellation of priorities, a redirected channeling of interests and devotions. We can take a challenge and transform it into an exciting opportunity.

November, 1971

DIASPORA ASSETS FOR JEWISH LIFE

Two centuries have elapsed since Canada became a part of the widespread Jewish Diaspora. In the course of these years, while preserving the fundamentals of their heritage, our people have become well and firmly integrated in their new Western setting. That they contributed to the growth and development of Canadian life at large is attested by all. Not only as individuals, but as Jews. Sometimes wittingly, sometimes unwittingly, they translated in many different ways the values and traditions of their great heritage into the burgeoning society round about them. We have used our Judaism to enrich Canadian life. We are grateful and happy for this privilege, and are resolved to continue to make the peculiar endowments of our people and culture an asset and blessing to our country.

We must not lose sight of the fact, however, that ours is a two-way traffic opportunity. If Judaism has much to offer the milieu in which we live, there is a great deal, too, in our Diaspora which can be of value and advantage for our modern Jewish life. Jewish history bears out the fact that in every time and in every clime Judaism was always a dynamic and open-end kind of culture, using with reason and care surrounding developments and influences for its own evolution. This is the give and take of civilization at its best, the interdependence of human society that spells progress.

It is true, historians can point to many analagous features which were common to all Diasporas. But there are differences and distinctions. Heine in his day could still be dazzled by the wealth of his Christian friends. Prosperity was something Christian and rare amongst Jews. That is not the case today, and especially in our Western hemisphere. I don't mean to give the impression, fancied and so frequently reiterated by anti-Semites, that wealth is concentrated in the hands of Jews. Far from it. But it is a true obser-

71

vation, I believe, that never before in history did the Jewish community as a whole enjoy the kind of material wherewithal that is ours here on the American continent. This is a new phenomenon in our history, a peculiar concomitant of our part of the Diaspora. Is it being put to proper use? I am well aware of the exemplary generosity of our people and, indeed, our story of philanthropy is a glorious chapter in any man's book. Nonetheless, one cannot escape the awareness that we here are not bringing the full weight of our material resources to bear upon the enhancement of our Jewishness.

Recently, the Council of Jewish Federations and Welfare Funds in the United States published a survey report on national Jewish cultural services in America. The report can have no argument with Jewish philanthropy in its conventional sense. It is, however, dismayed to note what a pittance is given for cultural and educational institutions in the Jewish community. The situation is no different in Canada. We are not using our newly-won asset of material security to create and support seminaries, Jewish colleges, Jewish researchers and scholars, Jewish libraries, chairs of Judaica at universities. Professor Salo Baron, speaking in my synagogue some years ago, made the statement that were we to develop fifty American Jewish scholars of first rank, we would change the face of all Jewish life on this continent. Here is a challenge we have not yet met, an opportunity that we have not exploited.

Ours is not only a unique opportunity in terms of material resources for the enhancement of our Judaism, but equally in terms of manpower potential. Never before in history have Jews at large been so integrated in and part of the wider secular culture round about them as they are today. I am not unmindful of other eras wherein our people shone in the worlds of science and art. The rich Hellenistic period in pre-Christian Alexandria, the Golden Age in medieval Moslem Spain, or even the days of the Renaissance in Italy, all come quickly to mind. But the fact is that in all these glorious periods, while Jews reached pinnacles of cultural and intellectual creativity in the non-Jewish milieu, they were for the most part single Jews. There was no broad base of full participation. This is precisely the difference. Today, especially in our scene, we are involved en masse in the broader world culture. The average Jew today is more culturally equipped and better educated than his counterpart in any time heretofore; never before have so many of our people gone on to such advanced areas of general learning and knowledge as in modern times. The tragedy is that we are not using this modern superiority for the inner streams of Jewish life. Undoubtedly, were we to exploit our unparalleled intellectual and cultural resources for our Jewishness, we could effectuate a Jewish renaissance that defies present imagination. Our challenge is to encourage Jews who are philosophers to become Jewish philosophers, Jews who are writers to become Jewish writers, Jews who are composers to become Jewish composers, Jews who are artists to become Jewish artists, even this much, to get the average Jew to approach his heritage with his new-won intellect and thus elicit from it a more insightful understanding and deeper appreciation.

Our trouble is not that we are "assimilated," but rather that we do not use our "assimilation" for the increment of our Judaism.

Here, finally, is another new experience of our Diaspora that we are not putting to sufficient use—the democratic process. Let no one take offense. It is true, as Judge Simon Rifkind phrased it some years ago, that "The basic axioms of democracy—human dignity, equality, and freedom—are all as Jewish as the Hebrew language." The basic spirit of democracy is not new with us; and yet we must admit that democracy, in our developed sense of that concept, is something that the Jew encountered for the first time when he emerged from the ghetto, and more especially when our people in great numbers came to these shores from Eastern Europe. Democracy is a big concept, but I have reference now to that phase of it which is described as unity in diversity. In our communal life, even more so in our religious life, we enjoy both unity and diversity, but all too frequently we don't enjoy them simultaneously. The religious champion wants unity and sees it in terms of uniformity; while the advocate of tolerance pushes diversity at the cost of unity. To pair them together, to have a community that is united in spite of its differences, is democracy at its practised best. It is something we would do well to incorporate in increasing measure within our Jewish life.

This is our challenge as Canadian Jewry goes forward into its third century of history. Let us by all means enrich our Canadian society with our Jewish values, and, at the same time, enhance our Judaism with our Canadian blessings.

February, 1962

TO FIX WHAT IS BROKEN

The Fixer. Whence this title? I haven't yet seen the film, but I did read Malamud's novel. In an interview with Haskel Frankel in the Saturday Review, Malamud explained the name of his book this way: "The title—well, it came to me from Corvallis, Oregon; I taught at Oregon State College before going to Bennington. There was a sign I would see almost every day—Jim the Fixer. That's where the title came from."

Is that really the explanation? Or is Malamud just putting Frankel on? The explanation doesn't seem to go to the core of the matter. In this same interview, Malamud says of his novel: "I don't want it tied to the Beiliss case . . . the story of Yakov Bok is an imaginative piece of work . . . You see, for me, the book has a mythological quality. It has to be treated as a myth, an endless story, more than a case study." In the light of the significance which the author himself would accord this book, one is the more strongly persuaded that there is a metaphoric and symbolic quality about the title. At the very least, psychoanalytically, *The Fixer* is a very pregnant title.

Who is this fixer named Yakov Bok? On one level, he is merely a fictional character, the hero of a story about injustice. Largely modelled after Mendel Beiliss, he is, as the author himself says, a composite character drawn from a Dreyfus, a Vanzetti, a Timothy Evans, or a Mendel Beiliss. Yet, on another level—in the mythological dimension of the story—Yakov Bok is more of a symbol and less of a particular person. Yakov, Jacob—here is a clear cut appellation for the Jew. Yakov means the Jew. Bok is Yiddish for a goat; and surely the allusion is patent, the scapegoat. Yakov Bok is Jake the goat; he is the Jew who is the scapegoat. The Jew is the classical scapegoat, the fall-guy of history. Yakov Bok symbolizes the Jewish people.

75

Now, perhaps, *The Fixer* can be seen in greater depth. In Jewish tradition, the Jew is envisaged as the *metaken olam bemalchut shaddai*, as the member of a people whose mission it is *letaken*, to correct, to repair, to perfect, to fix the world under the reign of the Almighty. This is Yakov's trade—this is the Jew's business —to be a fixer. "I fix what's broken," says Yakov. That's the Jew's job—to fix a world that is broken.

Can he? Is the world fixable? Will justice ever prevail? On his way to the trial at the end of the story, in his imagination Yakov heard the chairman of a jury selected from the lowest and most ignorant elements in society say: "A man learns to recognize the truth, even if he doesn't always live by it . . . The officials may not want us to know what the truth is; but it comes in, you might say, through the chinks in the walls. They may try to deceive us, as they do often enough, but we will sift the evidence, and if the facts are not as they say, then let them look to their consciences . . . You aren't born human for nothing I say."

"You aren't born human for nothing." For all the justified pessimism and cynicism, history would seem to say that our basic Jewish optimism and humanity are warranted, that the world is fixable, that in the long run right will prevail. Ultimately, the truth comes in, if need be, through the chinks in the wall. And until it does, we need the resolve and fortitude to persevere and not give in, the determination to hold out to be fixers.

February, 1969

THESE ARE THE FESTIVALS OF THE LORD

Leviticus 23:4

Mané-Katz: "Meditation"
From Mane-Katz by Alfred Werner, through the courtesy
of Massadah Publishing Ltd., Tel Aviv

THAT EXTRA PUSH

The story is told of the man who rushed down to the railroad station to catch the last train for New York, only to find the conveyance pulling out just as he reached the terminal gates. He began to wring his hands and lament his bad luck. Now he really was in a predicament. It was so crucially important for him to make that train. What was he to do? His visible consternation caught the eye of a bystander. "How late were you?" asked the fellow sympathetically. "Just about 30 seconds, that's all," he moaned. "Not more, eh?" said the bystander. "By the way you're carrying on, I thought it must have been by at least one hour." It is said that a miss by an inch is as bad as a miss by a mile. Even more so, for it is the more aggravating. The trains that we come so close to making and miss by a fraction, the almost but not quite, that's what rankles so. With but only a little more effort, with just an extra push, we'd have made it.

And the truth to be told, most of the trains we miss in life are lost by the smallest of margins. Out of Jewish tradition comes our conviction that the average man, far from being depraved and bereft of all decency, does have a strong inclination to the good. Conscience bespeaks that truth. There is no choice of doing the wrong thing but that in the process of deciding there was not also present the temptation to do the right thing. We usually miss out on our ethics not by a mile, only by an inch. We're almost good, but not quite. With just an extra push, we might have made it.

Think back now on the yesteryear, and are not our regrets compounded of that kind of stuff? We recall those moments when, in the trials of deciding, we were strongly minded to give, it was in us to come through, we were almost generous; but then, we didn't quite make it. The time we came so close to saying a kind word, there was reason for commendation, too; yet, instead, we emitted

81

a barbing one and let loose our urge to criticize. Those intimate occasions when we nearly struck a faster relationship with our children, only to allow our good intentions to buckle under at the last moment and be swerved by some other preoccupation. That's what galls us so—the close parents we almost were, but didn't quite prove to be. Now, in retrospect, this hurts. Our honesty that lost out to expediency only by a hairbreadth of temptation. Our aversion to prejudice that surrendered to the bigotry of the crowd. That's what aggravates—almost character, but not quite. With a jot more persistence, we might have made it.

And how good, too, we might have been not only to others, but to ourselves as well. So many were the times we toyed with giving our abilities a better chance, but, at the testing moment, gumption failed us. Adversity has a way of making us think more profoundly and invests us with a broader set of values. Trouble instructed us, and how close we were to becoming new individuals bent on living a more sensible life; yet, with recovery, we are our old selves again. To be sure, we all can't be saints and scholars. Is there, however, a Jew so obtuse that he does not inwardly wish to grow spiritually and be a more integrated member of his people and the human race? The opportunity is his. If not everywhere in the world today, here at least, we can worship as we would, study what we will, think as we please. Is this part of the complex of our regrets, all those opportunities of the synagogue and the Jewish community that were so close at hand yet we somehow missed out on? That's what hurts, almost a better Jew, but not quite. With just a little extra push, we might have made it.

This is the season that calls forth honest regrets for our failures of yesteryear. More so, however, does it awaken the conviction that past errors need not be repeated and the resolution to repair our foibles. In all piety we shall soon pray *Hayom te'amtsenu*, O Lord, give us strength. May, indeed, ours be the strength, in the coming year, to exert just a little more effort and forfend all galling regrets. May ours be the fortitude to make it.

Rosh Hashanah, 5724

DON'T PIDDLE LIFE AWAY

At the turn of the year, we are inevitably seized with a sense of the transiency of time. Life is not only fleeting, it is so short. "So teach us to number our days," prayed the Psalmist, "that we may get us a heart of wisdom." It's a sin to waste the years. Heart and mind tell us—don't piddle your life away.

Living as we do in affluent times, it's quite easy to wax wasteful. "Waste not, want not," is no longer a valid adage for us, writes Joseph Wood Krutch. Rather, "waste or you will want" is one of the most fundamental truths in the new Rich Richard's Almanac. Luxury is the innocent term we employ, but it doesn't really hide the fact that we are operating today with a perverted sense of values vis-à-vis our substance and means. We use our wealth for trivialities and vulgarities. Our wastefulness becomes all the more sharply delineated when we contrast the things we do with our means with the things we fail to do. More often than not ours is a prodigality for goods and things we don't need, and a comparative frugality and parsimony for things that are eminently more worthwhile. Isn't it paradoxial that in the richest Jewish community of history, climbing the walls as it were to find new ways of conspicuously squandering its substance, seminaries have to go begging for support, and scholarship still remains frustrated by a lack of funds. How did someone put it to me the other day—"We have a Cadillac taste with a Ford pocket." I could understand the stricture were it not for the Cadillac pockets we have for a host of inconsequentials. Are we really making the best use of our means? Do we waste it just on ourselves and on our materialistic pleasure, or do we use it more tellingly to enlarge the happiness around us and to do something genuinely worthwhile with our lives? Even if it's only money, it's a sin to waste it.

Our intellectual capacities are amongst our most precious assets.

83

What a shame to piddle them away. Using intellect just to be a smart alec, using it just to parade a stance of cleverness and brilliance, sporting around intellectuality, instead of using it as an impetus to truth and as a guide for sane and committed living— what a misuse of a God-given capacity! Have you noticed how some of our academicians excel in tearing things down with their mental prowess? No one objects to critical appraisal, but something is awry when all that wisdom adds up to is negativism and destructiveness. Here's a pretty grim statistic—ours is at one and the same time the most educated and one of the most corrupt generations in history. There is no correlation between our cultural and ethical indices. Surely we are guilty of the sin of wastefulness when our intellectuality is not producing better human beings. Whether it be the gift of mind or any other capacity, don't fritter it away.

No great betrayals, no great violations and infidelities, just whittling away our love and marriage. Of all life's stretches of wasteland, perhaps this is the saddest and most costly erosion. Someone called it the sin of perennial human blindness. Our family life, which might have proved to be so glorious and rewarding, is sapped of its potentials by the attrition of our jaded impatience, careless neglects, thoughtless crudities and coarseness, and stupid pettiness. What a sin to waste the great and incomparable gifts of love and kinship.

Perhaps in no area of our lives is our theme more relevant than in the domain of our Jewishness. Too many of us, in all candor, shamelessly and shamefully are wasteful of our Judaism. Observing rather than observant, we stand on the fringes of our heritage and are at best but spectators and not participants in Jewish living. More and more we tend to attenuate our faith into a mere identification tag, sometimes into a kind of psychological therapy for our own personal selfish needs. The great challenge inherent in our tradition, the demands it makes of us, the standards to which it would raise us, with these we have little truck. The best that is in our Judaism we wantonly overlook.

A New Year lies ahead of us. I turn to my readers with all the earnestness that I can muster and urge them to take new stock of their affiliation with the synagogue. That the synagogue is an incomparable reservoir of meaningful Jewish living for young and old, there is no denying. But it is more, too. In it we shall find the wisdom and the strength to live all of life as full human beings should live it. Your synagogue has a great deal to offer you. Don't waste it.

Rosh Hashanah, 5725

WITH MORE PASSION

"Inscribe us in the Book of Life."

Of all our orisons in the High Holy Days season, in all probability it is this one that commands our greatest fervor and sincerity. There's no gainsaying our passion for life, but there is reason, especially today, to question the passion wherewith we live. The listlessness, the ennui, the blaséness, the boredom that comprise the tenor of our contemporary ethos unmistakably asperse the excitement of our existence. My prayer and plea for the New Year is that we be more passionate in our living.

Strange, you say, that we should have to be urged to be more excited about living. Aren't the events of the hour in and of themselves sufficiently exhilarating? I suppose they are, but I am reminded of a keen observation made by Edmund Fuller in one of his books. Writes Mr. Fuller: "The state of being bored is subjective. Life is never boring, you are bored." There never really is occasion for indifference; and yet people are, notwithstanding all the reason for excitement, bored and blasé. If we want to experience and enjoy the excitement of life, then we must needs in our own persons exert more passion in our living.

What can we do to attune our inner beings to the excitement in life? I refer to Edmund Fuller again. "The new gullibility of our particular time," he allows, "is not that of a man who believes too much, but that of a man who believes too little, the man who has lost his sense of the miracle. When awe and wonder depart from our awareness, depression sets in; and after its blanket has lain smotheringly upon us for a while, despair may ensue or the quest for kicks begin. The loss of wonder, of awe, of the sense of the sublime, is a condition leading to the death of the soul. There is no more withering state than that which takes all things for granted."

To put more passion in our living—Mr. Fuller has spelled out the first prerequisite. It is a course, too, that is emphatically recommended by the celebrated Jewish philosopher and theologian, Dr. Abraham Heschel. It is imperative that we focus on the great mysteries of life and therewith become suffused with a sense of awe and wonder. How many of us ever do this—take time out to ponder on the great questions? "Be open-eyed," counsel the Rabbis, "to the great wonders of nature, familiar though they be. Men are more wont to be astonished at the sun's eclipse than at its unfailing rise." Is there, indeed, a corner in life that is not replete with cause for marvelling, whether it be the harmonies evident in nature, or the tantalizing reality of human consciousness, or the miracle of learning and communication? It's not that life can be wonderful; it is wonderful, if only we open our beings to the excitement round about us.

A second prerequisite would have us invest our endeavors and undertakings with a greater measure of enthusiasm. Of a lackadaisical couple dancing a minuet, Lord Chesterfield once remarked that they looked as if they were hired to do it, and were doubtful of being paid. What an apt description of so many of us in so many different areas of our daily existence. We go through the motions, but without any zeal, without any conviction. We meet our obligations and fulfill our roles, but only perfunctorily. No wonder our achievements are so pedestrian. This is true, isn't it, of our jobs, of our businesses, of our professions? True also in more decisive and important areas, our family life for example. Ben Hecht, in his book *A Child of the Century,* can write: "Love is real only for the young. The mature must look at it with wiser eyes, and see it for the many other things it is—selfishness, robbery, and the hiatus between deceits." Is this what love really is —boredom, selfishness, the hiatus between deceits—or is this rather what we allow love to dwindle into when we deprive our family relationships of the interest, concern and dedication wherewith we started? It is a high price we pay for sophistication when the pursuits of our existence wane into perfunctory routine.

Finally, may I urge that we put more passion in our living by stoking our sense of indignation. That we are capable of ire and anger, needs no saying. Scratch our egos, thwart our desires, and we're all aflame. That's not what I'm alluding to, however, when I speak of indignation. William Howard Taft once observed that too many people don't care what happens so long as it doesn't happen to them. It's precisely when it doesn't happen to us directly that indignation at its best shines forth. Getting angry about the injustices, the shoddiness, the wrongs that infest society; becoming hot and bothered about the deterioration of morality, corruption in government, prejudice and racialism, the waxing rate of intermarriage amongst Jewish youth—a sense of a cause and mission, that is the stuff that fills human existence with passion and generates meaning in life. Life can be exciting, if we are concerned and not blasé.

May the coming year find us all more passionate in our living.

Rosh Hashanah, 5726

THIS YEAR I'M IN EARNEST

People are more honest and realistic nowadays, someone was explaining to me the other day. That's why they no longer make resolutions, because they know they will not keep them. Hence it is that making resolutions for the New Year is fast becoming an outmoded practice. More often than not it's an empty ritual, a futile gesture, at best a momentary sop to good intentions. Isn't it better, then, isn't it less hypocritical and more honest—if you're not going to keep them—not to repeat those time-worn avowals? It's better not to vow, counsels Scripture, than to vow and not fulfill.

All hail to honesty. Yet, I am no little disturbed by this approach of realism, for all that it sounds the moral notes of truthfulness and integrity. To be sure, "the smallest good deed is better than the grandest good intention." Nonetheless, I am persuaded that the discontinuation of our registering of good intentions is, in a number of ways, a deleterious and grievous development.

Observes Rabbi Ammi in the Talmud: If someone so much as intended to do a good deed and was unable to fulfill it, Scripture credits him as though he had done it. The Sages of Yavneh were wont to say: It matters not whether you do much or little, so long as your heart is directed to heaven. Good intentions, avowed noble aims, New Year's resolutions—no matter how momentary, no matter how oft repeated, no matter how doubtful their realization— they are never fatuous and futile, not to mention hypocritical and dishonest.

Even when the odds are against your keeping them, make resolutions for the New Year. Make them because entertaining aspirations is a healthful experience to a human being. A person who is still titillated by the prospect of change and improvement serves notice, on himself as well as on others, that he is far yet from being done with, and that there still courses within him a spirit

89

of vitality. People who reject despair and self-surrender by looking ahead with resolve, people who yet have something to achieve in their own persons, people who even toy with the idea of changing for the better, such people are in a profound sense healthier individuals.

Make resolutions, because it is in the experiencing of aspirations and goals that a human being senses par excellence his freedom. "A man is free only when he has an errand on earth," wrote Rabbi Silver. How pungently put—we are precisely in the fullest and most satisfying exercise of our liberty when we set sights for ourselves and go after them. Resolutions are errands wherewith we commission ourselves; they are the stuff that invests us with a sense of freedom.

But not only a sense of freedom; even more so, a sense of meaning and purpose in life. It matters not altogether that we fail personally in achieving the goal. The very fact that we indulge in resolutions indicates that we are aware of a discrepancy between our behavior and the ideal, that we are propelled by a sense of ought. And if nothing else, if there be no more concrete results than just this—a sense of discrepancy, a sense of inadequacy, of failure—the game is worth the candle. For it is precisely a feeling of this sort, that there is in life something outside ourselves worth living up to, that informs us with an awareness of meaning and purpose in life. It was in this vein that the philosopher Henri Bergson could write, "It is the very essence of intelligence to undertake what it does not feel absolutely sure of carrying out."

And suppose you can't make it; suppose for one reason or another you can't live up to your resolutions. There is at least this about the situation which is of no little consideration: chances are, if resolutions are part of your scheme, that if you can't be all that you want to be, at least you won't become worse than you are. And who knows? Perhaps if you resolve long enough, if you persist in spite of all the past repeated failures, there may come a moment of breakthrough—a moment when you will not break your resolution, but rather, by virtue of your resolution, break through the obstacles and succeed.

Of Levi ben Yitzchak it is said that in his latter years be adopted the following practice: Each night on retiring he would review his day and say of whatever was evil in it, "I shall not do so again." Having said this, he would continue his soliloquy. "But so you promised last night and the night before." "Ah, yes," he would answer himself, "but tonight I am in earnest."

For all our past failures, I invite you on this eve of the New Year to join me in making New Year's resolutions.

Rosh Hashanah, 5727

EVERY EFFORT HAS ITS REWARD

In our personal lives, what shall we be praying for this Rosh Hashanah? Indubitably, we shall humbly and hopefully ask for many things. We are certainly not short of desires and ambitions; we are long on expectations. All of which reminds me of the teacher who asked her class what the difference was between results and consequences. "Results," a bright young lad suggested, "are what you expect; consequences are what you get." Are you praying this year for results?

A student once came complaining to the Hafetz Hayyim. "Rabbi," he said bitterly and dejectedly, "for many years now I have been wearying myself over the Torah, and I still haven't reached the stage when I can understand a page of the *Gemara* with its commentaries properly. For years I've sweated over the Torah, and there are no results." Whereupon the saintly Rabbi replied, "Young man, the good Lord never commanded us to become scholars and geniuses. We have only been enjoined to meditate in the Torah day and night. Let us labor over it regardless of whether or not we become proficient and erudite. Ours is merely to toil over it, irrespective of the results." There is wisdom here. Persist in your efforts even if you don't get results; for the fact of the matter is that, more often than not, we are wrong in feeling that there are no results. You can't strive, you can't exert effort, you can't work and try without engendering results.

Avers Rabbi Isaac in the Talmud that if somebody tells you that he labored and got nowhere, don't believe him. And the sage is right. When you cavil and carp that you work and work and get no results, by results you usually mean immediate and tangible results. Frankly, however, this attitude betrays a kind of arrogant impatience. Perhaps the goal you've set can't be accomplished by the application which you have given it, perhaps it can't be done in the time you've accorded it; perchance it calls for more toil, for more duration. To what may this be compared? To a man who set out by foot for a distant city. He walked and walked until he could walk no more, and still he didn't reach his destination. "I've tried," he cried, "I tried, but got nowhere." Surely you perceive the fallacy of his lament. True enough, he may not have reached his destination; but it's simply not factual to allow that he made no progress. No one who starts out for a destination can claim that he didn't get somewhere. No one who strives for a goal can say that he got no results.

Perhaps that's the way life is structured—goals are achieved only in piecemeal fashion. Shall we say of the researcher who has failed in experiment after experiment in the laboratory to get what he's after that he chalked up no results? It is axiomatic in the world of science that failures are but the stepping stones on which researchers reach their goals. Such is the economy of life that every seemingly futile attempt is efficacious and resultative. Isn't that what the Sages meant when they said that for every little effort we exert for holiness there is, unbeknown and unseen in the immediacy, ultimately a great and enduring reward? It's inescapable—you can't honestly try without generating some results.

Does someone complain that she has failed with her daughter, that he has gotten nowhere with his son? Methinks, from what I hear round about me, that many are the parents who are convinced of the futility of their efforts in child-rearing and are ready to "give up." They should be persuaded, these despairing and cynical sires, that their solicitude and attentions may not bear fruits now but augur well to blossom later. More often than not, later, when in turn they are more mature, our children come through for us and reflect the devotions we've invested in them. With a litle more patience, we do get results.

Is some young person beginning to sour on his academic pursuits? Reports indicate that the rate of attrition in our colleges is increasing and the phenomenon of dropouts is bestirring a growing concern. There seems to be a feeling abroad that so many of the intellectual disciplines offered on the campus are completely irrelevant and a "waste of time." There is something to be said for the pragmatic individual, but, in the long run of things, no cultural indulgence, nothing we've learned, is ever lost. For all its immediate intangibility, knowledge has a way of enlarging a personality and moulding a more complete human being.

Those of us who are engaged in the religious area of life are frequently discouraged by the paucity of results. It's one of the perennial refrains in the circles of Jewish education—there are no results. No results? The overwhelming manifestation of Jewish unity this past summer belies that allegation. We are much too quick, and in the long run unjustified, to conclude that we are getting nowhere.

Are you going to pray for results this Rosh Hashanah? I fear the focus is wrong. Results have a way of coming in their own time. And come they inevitably do, if only we persist. Let's rather pray, then, for the wisdom to work, the resolve to hew to our goals, and the strength to persevere—irrespective of results.

Rosh Hashanah, 5728

MAY YOU BELONG

This is the period in the year when all but the most errant among us are seized with a desire to belong. There is something about the High Holy Days season that calls us back to Jewish life and draws us nearer to the bosom of our people and faith. One hesitates to invoke the word *teshuvah*, a term so freighted with such piety and devoutness, glibly and without diffidence. I am not at all sure that what most of us experience in these Days of Penitence is *teshuvah* in the real religious sense of contrition and repentance. But in its original and simpler meaning, in the sense of returning, *teshuvah* is not too pretentious a word wherewith to convey the state of our emotions. For all our callous indifference to Judaism during the year, come Rosh Hashanah, and there is a compelling urge to repair the estrangement. It matters not how far we strayed the last twelvemonth, come these Days of Awe, and we make a volte-face. We want to get back. We want to feel that we do belong. Once again we want to be belonging Jews.

But wishing will not make it so. Belonging is more than a matter of desire. It's a matter of fulfilling the inner meanings that are implicit in the word itself.

Belonging carries with it the implication of worthiness. When a membership committee evaluates an applicant and says that he belongs, it means, of course, that the individual measures up to the required standards and deserves to be affiliated. What we are obviously stressing is not association but merit of association. It was recently said of an American legislator that he belonged to the Senate but not in it. The crucial question is not do you belong to a synagogue, but do you belong in a synagogue. The vast majority of us want to associate ourselves with the great achievement of Israel which we have been privileged to behold in our day, often unmindful that being a member in the Zionist movement is not altogether

95

synonymous with being a Zionist. This is the season when we want to be belonging Jews. Let us remember, however, that this desire is meaningless and futile unless we, by virtue of the ethical life that we lead, the Torah that we study, the *mitzvot* that we observe, and the communal responsibilities that we discharge, show that we qualify to belong.

And belonging implies self-surrender. Surely we've noticed, in ourselves as well as in others, the ironic tendency to belong to an institution and then behave as if the institution belonged to us. There are times when we must remind ourselves that, for all the demands we as members have a right to make upon the community for our interests, ours in the last analysis is to yield to the common weal and not the common weal to us. The most religious among us are not always beyond an attitude which suggests that God belongs to them and not they to God. How often we must try to convince some of our people that making Judaism part of their life does not mean fitting Judaism into their scheme of things but the converse, fitting their scheme of things into the framework of our faith and tradition. This is the season when we want to be belonging Jews. Let us remember, then, that it is only when we are humble enough to surrender our personal sovereignty to the totality of Jewish life, it is only when we act by the proposition that we belong to Judaism, and not Judaism to us, that our desire will see fruition and we will belong.

Rosh Hashanah, 5729

DON'T WRITE YOURSELF OFF

I have been lambasting you, *musaring* and berating you, for years now. But truthfully, in this season of stock-taking in depth, I wouldn't want you to feel that you are all that bad.

I think we would all agree with the Hebrew writer Jacob Klatzkin when he said, "He who cannot at times hate himself or despise himself must needs be lacking in conscience." When it's a matter of judging ourselves, there are instances when we sorely need a more acutely sensitized conscience which will disenchant us with ourselves and make us realize that we're not all that good. There is merit in our Sages' admonition to be lacking in our own sight. That, however, is one side of the coin. On the other side, Rabbi Simeon goes out of his way to counsel us to be moderate in our self-denigration and not to account ourselves wicked in our own sight. Don't think overly much of yourself; but, on the other hand, neither should you think too little of yourself.

You know well enough that you are far from being a model parent. Granted, not a model parent, but don't convince yourself, as I constantly hear fathers and mothers try to do, that you are a failure as a parent. You're not all the Jew you might be, Jewishly you're lacking? True enough, but you're not as bad a Jew as you would persuade yourself to be. God knows, in so many ways ours is not the finest of generations. Rabbi Simeon, however, would forfend us from stigmatizing ours as the worst of ages. Make no mistake about it. The Rabbi is no advocate of pride and vanity, but he does reject self-deprecation and self-contempt.

And with good reason. In the first instance, we know psychologically today that self-derogation is often in reality a disingenuous form of vanity, a kind of hypocritical preoccupation with the self. Spinoza sensed this phenomenon when he remarked, "One who despises himself is the nearest to a proud man." It is with good

97

reason that Rabbi Simeon abjures our indulgence in self-contempt. Who do you think you are, he is angrily saying, that you should focus so much on yourself and make yourself out to be so bad?!

Psychologically sound, and the Rabbi is on strong ethical grounds as well. It is morally bankrupting to disparage yourself. Very often as a man thinks of himself, so will he be. We conjure up an image of ourselves, and then we fill the role of that image. A man tells himself that he's a mean and severe kind of a boss, and then he proceeds to settle for that character. Never consider yourself wicked, advises Maimonides, for by so doing you give up hope of repenting and changing, and become confirmed in your wickednes. A person who tells himself that he is a failure closes the door of hope in his own face and puts himself out of the running. It's an unwarranted act of surrender. I'll never learn, so why break my head? I'll never score, so why all the effort? Rabbi Simeon dislikes the self-belittling individual, because the latter defeats himself even before he tries.

Sometimes it's even more pernicious and sinister. Sometimes minimizing oneself is a sly way out, a disguised alibi for an escape. Admit that you are a failure, and then no one will expect anything more from you. Tell yourself that it's no use denying it, you are a tempestuous individual that's all; and how wonderful, you've excused yourself from an exertion of self-control. Confess that you have a weakness for the opposite sex and infidelity is your peccadillo, and you've endowed yourself with a permanent *hechsher*. Rabbi Simeon won't buy it. He's minded that you're not such a dyed-in-the-wool reprobate that you can't improve and be better than you are.

Finally, there is this overriding consideration—you can't have contempt for yourself and still carry respect and love for others. For me, the profounder implication of the Biblical "Thou shalt love thy neighbor as thyself" is that, in order for me to be able to love my neighbor, I must first be able to love myself.

In this sense, self-love is not a manifestation of selfishness. It is, rather, the root experience which, when projected, makes it possible for me to love and respect and care for others. The tragedy of the self-contemptuous Jew is not alone that he hates himself and his people, but also that he hates everyone. A self-hater is not capable of any affection. The fanatic who has no regard for himself, make no mistake about it, has no regard for any human being. A generation that despises itself is a generation which has no use for any age in history. That's the whole and significant point of the social scientist's observation, "It is not love of self but hatred of self which is at the root of the troubles that afflict our world." Rabbi Simeon is justly wary of self-condemnation. He would have us possess a litle more consideration for the society in which we live, and therefore be not wicked in our own sight.

During the coming Holy Days period, you will be taking an honest look at yourself. I trust that you are going to find faults. Don't, however, commit the worst of faults—especially in the season of *teshuvah,* don't write yourself off.

Rosh Hashanah, 5730

THE FUTILITY OF ISOLATIONISM

A man's house is his castle.

So wrote Sir Edward Coke, one of England's greatest lawyers, back at the beginning of the seventeenth century. While he offered the dictum primarily for its legal implications, the eminent jurist was not unaware of the larger connotation which attaches to it. Thus, he appended to it a quotation from the Roman writers, *et domus sua cuique tutissimum refugium*—"one's home is the safest refuge to everyone."

A man's home is his castle.

At least, that's what we would like to believe. Whatever concurrence the asseveration won down through the years, it appears to me, if I gauge our mood correctly, it is more and more becoming a popular and even strident conviction in our midst. We would have it that the home is our protection. And this development is but another expression of the waxing isolationism of our times.

Many are the ingredients which have gone into the stew of our neo-isolationism. The influence of the ego-focused psychological sciences, the headlong pursuit after unfettered personal freedom and individualism, the whole thrust of contemporary pragmatism and the self-oriented philosophies—have all had a share in desocializing modern man and narrowing his horizon and interest. Perhaps even more puissantly consequential in this inward *drang* has been the revolutionary character of our times. Alvin Toffler, in his *Future Shock*, premises the thesis that the nervous system of the average individual simply cannot cope with the velocity and scope of the radical changes which are reshaping our milieu, and therefore is in shock. Irrefragably, ours is—politically, socially, technologically, and culturally—one of the most mutating of civilizations. For many, it's all too much to endure. Out of sheer despair, we are propelled to retreat behind our own little walls. Let the world go

100

its way—we'll preserve our own world by isolating ourselves in our own safe backyard. Society at large is too much for us. We'll make our home our castle and take care of our own.

A man's home is his castle. We would like to believe that. How comforting to feel that we can hole up in our own domain and withstand the undoing realities round about us. I'm afraid, however, that for all that it is a wish devoutly to be desired, it is only that— wishful thinking, an escapist illusion, and nothing more. There are no unassailable fortresses today. There is no home so encapsulated and impregnable that it can resist the sway of the culture of its context.

I hear it frequently from parents, and from fellow rabbis and ministers and counsellors, too. Never mind what's going on; concentrate on your own home, and you and the kids will come through unscathed. I am the last to question the primary need for every effort to preserve the values and wholesomeness of the family ambit. But I should be less than truthful were I to feel that that tack alone can succeed. There is too much heartache around testifying that a home on its own is no insulation against the ugly forces regnant in the wider milieu.

You can't isolate yourself. If you are worried about drugs and deviant lifestyles, about violence and immorality, about Jewish anti-Zionism and self-hatred, about intermarriage, about the whole galaxy of enormities which threaten you and your family—then, of necessity, your concern must be not only for your own, but for society at large. You can't make your home a castle.

This realism is imbedded in the very nature of the High Holy Days. No festival focuses more inwardly upon the individual than does Rosh Hoshanah. Yet, at the same time, it speaks consistently, in awesome cosmic terms, of man's integral role in the universe itself. It's not a home that is man's castle; it's the quality of the world he lives in that is his fortress.

Look after your own? By all means. But to do that effectively, you must needs exercise a broader concern and labor for the community of man.

Rosh Hashanah, 5732

THE LADDER OF PATIENCE

Don't set your sights too high.

All of us are familiar with this kind of counsel that issues from a spirit of realism and down-to-earthness. It would seem to me, however, that the danger does not lie in aiming too high, but rather in expecting achievement too soon.

Franz Kafka, in his *Reflections*, speaks of impatience as one of the two cardinal sins from which all others derive. What a profound insight! We don't lack ideals. We have ideals to begin with; but, because of our impatience in realizing them, we become discouraged and abandon them. We don't lack faith. We start with faith; but, because of a want of endurance, we become frustrated and cynical. We don't lack ability. We have ability; but, because of our over-eagerness, we despair and sink into indolence. The trouble is not that our goals are too high; the fault lies in our unwillingness to accord these goals time while they are in the making.

Recently, in response to the question whether he believed in the Darwinian theory, a professor said he certainly did. "As a matter of fact," he went on to say, "I am inclined even to go farther than Darwin did and believe that man has started on the return journey."

In all quarters today there is the tendency to demean man and downgrade our expectations of him. This proclivity is a hasty conclusion born of impatience and its concomitant discouragement. King David, at one period, fell into a similar trap. "I said in my haste," declared the royal Psalmist, "All mankind is a failure." Granted, when you are in haste, there is round about us enough evidence that the human creature is a lowly being. Yet, a more patient evaluation of man would breed the understanding that, if the human being has not reached the high sights which the Jewish tradition has set for him, he is at least on his way and making progress. If there is any hope for our world, then we need above all else the conviction to keep the sights high and the forebearance to allow man time to realize his full human potentialities. Professor Mordecai Kaplan is wont to observe that we are still only candidates for humanity. In a profound sense, nothing is more important than to have patience with mankind.

Are you the type that demands a finished product, or can you abide with tolerance someone who is still only on his way? Your employees, the young professional, the novice board member—do you make allowances for their inexperience and their inadequacy, or do you show them the disdain of your impatience? Are you in a huff about our young people? I am frequently aggravated by them too. Such skeptics, such heretics! What arrogance, what rudeness! Truthful reflection, however, will remind us that essentially it's all part of growing up, adulthood in the making. You don't jump from childhood to maturity in one leap. There is no need to abandon our expectations—only to harbor more patience and understanding for our young people who are on their way.

It would be foolhardy to aver that marriage is always workable. There are instances when the venture has been a mistake. But more often than not, it strikes me, the error is not in getting married, but in the impatience to perceive that it takes time to reach full happiness in wedded life. Especially in this fast and rapid era of ours, when the statistics on family breakdown have become so frightening, more young couples have to be impressed with the inevitable gradualism of life. You don't hastily relinquish dreams tried by the challenge of reality; you persevere, and, with the aid of time and wisdom, reach the aspired heights.

With a new year around the corner, let us not be afraid to set high goals for ourselves. But, along with our resolutions, let us take for ourselves a healthy measure of patience. Only then will our resolutions be accorded a fair chance. "No great thing," said the philosopher "is created suddenly anymore than a bunch of grapes or a fig. If you tell me you desire grapes, I answer you, there must be time."

Rosh Hashanah, 5734

TESHUVAH IS MORE THAN REPENTANCE

Repentance means contrition, remorse, feeling sorry enough to quit. *Teshuvah* entails something in addition. Of someone who repents, listen to what the Yiddish so pointedly says: It avers that *er tut teshuvah*. One doesn't simply repent, one *does* repentance. It has the ring almost of a program, of a course of action. In the Jewish scheme of things, repentance is an activistic concept. The connotation is imbedded in the Hebrew term as well. *Teshuvah* literally suggests a going back, a doing in the opposite direction. In our book, to repent, it's not enough to stop; one must do something of an antipodal nature. It's not enough to stop the trangressing; one must backtrack and engage in a countervailing *mitzvah*. It involves the element of compensation. You just don't feel sorry and quit your bad deed; you do something of an opposite stripe to make up for it.

You do that, you compensate for your failing, because, for one thing, it's a moral dictate. The sense of justice demands that you make good for what you have damaged and destroyed. You just don't feel sorry and stop your misdeed; rather you go on and make up for it, because a sense of morality impels an exercise of compensation.

And secondly, you compensate for your fault because it's an existential necessity. If you want to eliminate a culpable proclivity, then you have to train yourself in an opposite tendency. Thus you just don't stop a bad habit; you counteract it with a good habit. habit.

Standing outside the funeral parlor some weeks ago, a fellow Kohen philosophized—as one tends to do standing at that spot—and said to me: "You know, Rabbi, it's very true. Money isn't everything. How long should one run after the dollar?" Is there someone who is as good as his philosophy and has decided to call quits to his materialism? Listen, you just don't stop, you just don't retire from running after the dollar. You set in motion a whole different kind of life. You become interested in matters that were almost strange to and removed from you—culture, communal service, religion. You just don't stop being so materialistic. You have to counter it and become more spiritualistic.

What is it you want to get over? Perhaps it's that noisome hypercritical streak in you. Well, it won't do merely to shut up and refrain from all comment. You have to change your whole approach. Instead of finding faults, on which to latch and berate, you must needs seek out the commendable realities which you can compliment. Someone very badly needs to repair his grouchiness—he casts a pall of gloom on his family every evening when he comes home. But the point is, one doesn't just stop being a grouch; one has to go out of his way to be pleasant and a source of brightness in his setting.

"Once my solitude was thoroughly proved, I could surrender to the charms of a virile self-pity," says the narrator in Camus' story *The Fall*. The charms of self-pity. How many of us all too often are ensnared by those allures. Reverses have set in, and we feel terribly sorry for ourselves. Life has been unkind and has deprived us of someone we loved so much. We have reason and reason to feel sorry for ourselves. In spite of everything that we have sacrificed, the child we doted on has turned in the wrong direction. Who can blame us for feeling bitter? Someone is capable and has worked very hard for his desired goal, but circumstances beyond his control have thwarted his ambition and have robbed him of his chosen career. No wonder his frustration and dispirited surrender.

But rationally we know it butters no parsnips to brood and languish in self-pity. Thus we're deciding from here on in we're not going to mope and feel sorry for ourseves. Hat's off to you. Don't be angry, however, when I say—it's not enough. It's not enough to stop pitying yourself. You've got to do more. You must needs now become tough and demand of yourself.

For the coming year, let's do it the Jewish way—*Teshuvah*, and not just repentance.

Yom Kippur, 5733

THE BLESSING OF GRATITUDE

I think we all recognize that we ought to be grateful for our blessings. What we frequently overlook, however, is that to be grateful is a sure way to create blessings.

Consider, for example, how the trait of thankfulness has a way of deepening and enriching our lives. Jewish tradition reminds us that it is meet for a person to recite one hundred blessings every day. Round about us, there are constantly innumerable benefactions which are glibly overlooked because of our dulled sense of appreciation. The spirit that is awake and alive with gratitude inevitably elicits more enjoyment and happiness out of the daily round of existence. Out of the ordinary day, it makes a festival; out of the common event, a thrill. It is the most puissant antidote to ennui, a never-failing invitation to zestful living.

It is related that when the artist Donatello refused to accept a block of marble from a quarry in Florence because it was imperfect, Michelangelo took the rejected stone and carved from it his famous statue of David. Opportunity rarely comes fully equipped. The art of achievement lies in an appreciation for any and all of the raw materials of existence, however inadequate they sometimes seem to be. Somehow, when you are grateful instead of carping, life offers up a more promising yield.

Dostoevski once wrote: "A man who bows down to nothing can never bear the burden of himself." Egocentrism, isolation and loneliness, alienation—that surely is one of the heaviest and most grinding of loads. And note, in almost every instance the lonely people are those individuals who are sparing with their gratitude. It is only when we release our appreciation, when we bow down to something other than ourselves, that we create bonds which associate us with a world much wider than our own small selves. You can't

106

be a grateful kind of person without creating warmer relationships, without engendering a feeling of fellowship and belonging.

Succoth is, in essence, a festival of thanksgiving. Can we use it to enhance the capacity of gratitude in us? Be grateful for your blessings, but bless yourself, too, with gratitude.

Succoth, 5727

THE UNFINISHED MITZVAH

"And I smiled to think God's greatness flowed around our incompleteness."

Elizabeth Barrett Browning's wonderful line comes to me as I enter the *succah*. No matter how you decorate it and dress it up, the *succah* remains so patently and palpably unfinished and incomplete. And methinks that is no accident, but rather by design. Its undoneness is built-in by the *halachah*. You might put it this way: the virtue of the *succah* is the virtue of the unfinished. The whole observance seems to say that at times it's a *mitzvah* to undertake the unfinished.

Like the gumption, when something is overwhelmingly worthwhile, to start it, even if you don't know how you are going to complete it. Like the ability of remaining open and receptive, and not insisting that ours is the last word. Like the perspicacity to appreciate that success is not arrival, but only an intermediate stage in a never ending challenge.

Let me, however, focus the *mitzvah* of the unfinished upon one sphere in particular now. The dyspeptic but uncompromisingly truthful philosopher, Morris Raphael Cohen, phrased it boldly: "Neither in love nor in work, neither in society nor in solitude, neither in the arts nor in the sciences will the world of actuality permit us to attain perfection." The pursuit after perfection is a fatuous striving in a world which inescapably must remain incomplete and imperfect.

Yet, for all that truth, how intolerant most of us can be. How inconsiderate, in this respect, we can be of others. How impatient I frequently find myself with the imperfect Jew. How unrealistic a wife can be, sitting in my study complaining about her imperfect husband. How painfully disappointed parents can be in their less than perfect children. How hostile and frightening young people

108

can be in the face of their faulted parents and in the face of the limping system. As if there were a perfect Jew, or a perfect husband, or perfect parents, or a perfect system!

As if there could be a perfect self. They tell of the president of the firm who stood talking to the head of his electrical shop when a stranger walked up to them. The latter stated that he was an electrician and had heard there might be an opening. He went on at great length about his qualifications, repeatedly emphasising that he never, never made a mistake. Before the foreman could say a word, the president spoke up. "Sorry, mister, but I have three thousand men working at the plant, and they make at least three thousand mistakes a day. It wouldn't do at all to hire a man who never makes a mistake."

He boots us little good—the intolerant individual who demands perfection of himself. His exaggerated standards automatically hinder him from lending his efforts to society round about him. If he can't do it well, he won't do it at all; with the result that most of the time he doesn't do it at all. What an impossibly bereft world ours would be if everyone adopted an all-or-nothing attitude. We need the *succah* paradigm of coming to terms without limited talents and operating with the unfinished and imperfect. There is much to Edward Hale's lines:

> I am only one
> But still I am one.
> I cannot do everything
> But still I can do something.
> And because I cannot do everything
> I will not refuse to do the something that I can do.

Succoth, 5730

OURS ARE THE BLAME AND CLAIM

The world is mine, too.

He doesn't say so in so many words, but, in a sense, that's what the Jew dramatizes on Succoth. He holds his *lulav* in his hand, and, in an encompassing circuit, he waves it northward, eastward, southward, westward, heavenward and earthward. To whomever else it belongs, he is virtually saying, the world is mine, too.

That's something we have to remember when we are inclined to grow self-righteously indignant and critically lament the state of things. I am reminded of the individual who questioned his tailor's wanting to take a month to make him a suit when God fashioned the whole world in only six days. "Sure," said the tailor, "but have you taken a look at the world lately?" There's no gainsaying that the quality isn't all that it might be, that the fit leaves much to be desired. All is not as it should be. Neither is there any contending here that we are to be faulted for all that is wrong. But having allowed for this much exculpation, there are still large areas where we are inculpated. As if the fault were all another's and we had no hand in it!

We bemoan the sight of a democracy being torn apart by racial strife. We are distressed when we behold civilized societies ravaged by criminality and violence. What a crazy and terrible world, we lament. As if through our omissions and commissions we didn't help brew the poisonous stew! As if, in so many different ways, we didn't help create the deleterious generation gap which is undermining our civilization! We are dismayed by the immoralization of our milieu. As if we had nothing to do with setting patterns which led a whole younger generation astray! We bewail the ominous decline of Judaism in our midst and are haunted by the spectre of the pending disappearance of our faith and Jewish identity. To be sure, in part it is the consequence of historical forces.

110

But listen, the world is ours, too, and not only history's domain. If Judaism is in a steep and rapid decline, it's because of our Jewish insincerity and neglect, it's because of our folly and distorted priorities in Jewish community endeavors. Let's be honest. If there is. something rotten with the world, it's because there's something rotten with us in a very crucial way. The world is not only God's and history's, it's ours, too.

It sounds a note of accusation—the world is mine, too. But it also underlines a note of rights and encouragement. Because the world is mine, too, I have a place in it, and have every right, nay, every duty, to assert myself.

It has been observed that "He who allows himself to be a worm must not complain if he's trodden upon." Some of us must needs do less carping and more asserting. We establishmentarians, God knows, aren't always innocent, and we have a lot of mending to do, but neither are we thoroughly and fundamentally askew. We have every bit as much of a stake in the world as the counter-culturists, and probably a great deal more. By what logic and ethic are we establishmentarians—parents, religionists, rationalists, moralists, democrats—shamefully playing the worm and passively allowing ourselves to be trodden upon? For all its lacunae, the civilization we have evolved is a precious achievement. And it ill befits us now, through silence and idleness and self-effacement, to surrender to sinister and destructive counterforces and allow it to go to pot. After all, this is our world, too.

Succoth, 5732

THE PERSONAL TOUCH

The *mitzvah* lies in putting up the *succah* yourself.

Max Reinhardt once urged the leading star in his play to "put more life into his living." It strikes me that off stage as well as on stage we must needs do that, too. And one of the best ways to put more life into our living is to invest our relationships with a greater measure of personal involvement.

Joseph Wood Krutch characterizes us as "generous materialists." By and large, we are not selfish; we do not live for ourselves alone. We are a giving people. But here is the rub—we are generous with our material wherewithal and give liberally of what we have; we are not nearly as magnanimous, however, when it comes to giving of ourselves. We balk at getting involved personally.

And what is the result? We deprive the recipients of our generosity of that something which is infinitely more important than the things we give them—human concern and love. And secondly, we perpetrate an injustice against ourselves. We deprive ourselves of a sense of connection and a feeling of relatedness. Our whole relationship becomes tenuous and takes on a gossamer quality. The thrust of the *succah* law is altogether pointed. It would seize us with the realization that the essential matter is personal involvement.

The greatest rewards in education, for instructor and pupil alike, issue from a teacher who gives his children not only his skill and knowledge, but something of his person, too; from a teacher who is not only doing his job faithfully, but is, as well, personally involved with his children. This is true of all the service professions, of the minister, of the lawyer, of the social worker. Listen to some tell it, and it needs be said especially of the physician in these days of medicare. It's not enough to give what one is trained for, one's skill and knowledge and ability; one must put more life into his living and give of his personal care and concern as well.

112

No one wants to carp about our philanthropic traits. All power to us for our charitableness. The fact remains, however, that sometimes our help would be more valued if it were less of a material quality and more of a personal nature. Sometimes, people don't need our money; they need us. Of course, it's not always pleasant, perhaps it's even difficult, to become involved. But ofttimes, it doesn't suffice to allow generosity to exhaust our kindness, and we must needs put more life into our living.

Have you seen the cartoon where a small boy at the piano says to his mother, "Gosh, mummy, I wish you hadn't been deprived of so many things as a child!" There's no gainsaying the liberality of most parents with their children. We indulge them lavishly with all kinds of things, but the fact remains that things, for all the munificence of their measure, are no substitute for personal warmth and relationship. One gets the impression that nowadays many a parent, in spite of his goodness, is not personally involved in the world of his children to the degree that he might be. In the complex of our family, we can distil a greater reward by putting more of our own life into our living.

There is always an easy way of doing things. To be sure, you can get a *succah* put up and decorated for you. But that defeats the guts of the *mitzvah*. It's the personal touch that really counts. It is only when there is something of your own person in it that a *mitzvah* becomes meaningful and rewardingly a good deed.

Succoth, 5733

WHAT WILL IT GET US?

If there is any epithet that describes our society, it is the adjective "practical."

Standing with our two feet firmly on the ground, our most valued touch-stone is usefulness. Reared on a philosophy of pragmatism and imbued with a utilitarian spirit, we have scant patience for the unproductive, little tolerance for that which is not tangibly functional and useful. The deciding consideration almost always boils down to this—what can you do with it, what good is it?

There is no gainsaying the tremendous and even immeasurable results of our basic practicality. But having acknowledged the obvious and irrefutable, I am nonetheless aware that our thoroughgoing pragmatism is at times impoverishing and depriving. I am persuaded that our efficiency is not an unmixed blessing.

Theoretically, we have every reverence for all the fine affections of the human race, but in the fabric of our daily living and behavior, more often than not, it seems to dissipate and give way to what we euphemistically call the dictates of realism. Friendship is indeed one of the noblest expressions of man, but you have to be practical and look after yourself first. Someone remarked to me the other day that kindness was all right in a sermon; in real life, however, you don't get anywhere, unless you're tough. Everyone's for morality in our dealings, but business is business. Idealism is such a commendable quality, but be careful, you've got to keep a level head and not let yourself be carried away. To be sure, we profess the decent thing; but when all is said and done, our choice is usually determined by the very practical consideration of "what will it get us."

Very frankly I neither espouse nor admire overly much the *luftmensch* mentality. I agree, as adults we ought to be productive members of society and useful to our milieu. This is not to suggest,

114

however, that our education should be, as it is increasingly becoming, wholly and exclusively utilitarian. Observers close to the scene lament the fact that our university graduates, while more skilled than ever before in their chosen occupations, are at the same time less educated than heretofore and constitute the phenomenon of uncultured professionals. The consideration of *tachlis*, both on the part of the students and sometimes even more on the part of the parent, is eroding and vitiating the tradition of a liberal arts education. For all his utilitarianism, or perhaps because of his utilitarianism, John Stuart Mill felt compelled to write: "Men are men before they are lawyers, or doctors, or manufacturers; if you make them capable and sensible men, they will make themselves capable and sensible lawyers and doctors." I'm not sure where it gets one, but is a Jewish education to be valued merely for its practical consequences? Is training for the rabbinate the only motivation for higher Jewish study?

It's a very telling phrase, the one we recite about the Hanukkah candles: "These lights are sacred throughout the eight days of Hanukkah and we are not permitted to make any practical use of them." There are things in life that have a way of brightening our existence for all their impracticality.

Hanukkah, 5727

AND WHEN THERE IS FREEDOM?

The perversity of the human being!

Walking in the country, Douglas Jerrold, the famous English wit, was in the habit of plucking a buttercup and remarking, "If this would cost a shilling a root, how beautiful it would be!" Jerrold's observation goes not only to the root of the flower, but to the root of human nature itself. By and large people value a thing more if they have to pay for it than if they receive it for nothing. It's the psychology of cost—the more costly, the more desirable in our sight. And conversely, of course—the less costly, the less prized in our esteem.

It's this human trait that points up the story behind our own English word "want." The primary meaning of that verb is to lack, to be without. We say, for example, of an indecorous service that it wants dignity. To want basically means to be without. Yet see how this word is most commonly used today. For all intents and purposes it is the synonym par excellence for the word "desire." It's a kind of commentary—as if to say that we desire something, we want something, precisely because we do not have it. And concomitantly, when we have it, somehow our desire for it evaporates.

There is something else here, too. One is prompted sometimes to question the genuineness and sincerity of the desire. The impression is that we are more interested in the chase than in the catch. Aren't we readier to fight for a cause than to exercise the privilege once it is gained? We seem to get more kick out of parading in a demonstration than in utilizing the victory.

Here we are at the Festival of Hanukkah. I have always felt that a great injustice has been perpetrated against this holiday by considering it a minor festival. The fact is that Hanukkah should have pertinence not only for Jews, but for civilized peoples everywhere;

116

for the story of this holiday is nothing less than the story of the first struggle in history for the freedom of religion. And as Jews, we were compelled, in one guise or another, to repeat that battle again and again. Indeed, down to the very threshold of our own age, we have been history's classical contenders for religious liberty. How great, how beyond computation has been the price of religious freedom that we paid through the generations. "If there be ranks in suffering," wrote Leopold Zunz, "Israel takes precedence over all the nations."

But thankfully, that's all over, at least in our neck of the woods. Freedom of religion is a firmly established principle, an unquestionable reality in our society. We don't have to fight any more to worship when, where and as we please. Yet, precisely now when it is so easy to be religious, the majority of us are clearly less than excited about exploiting this privilege. We are hotter for the right to light a Hanukkah candle than for the opportunity to kindle it. We are agitated by the lack of religious freedom of our brethren in Russia—and rightfully so—but are dishearteningly indifferent to the faith we are free to observe here. It's easier to get our young people to demonstrate against synagogue restrictions in the Soviet Union than to go to *shul* here.

The words of Zechariah come to mind in this season. "Not by might, nor by power, but by My spirit, saith the Lord of hosts." Can I paraphrase it this way: don't be perverse—be Jews not only when you have to fight and battle for the freedom of your religion; more importantly, be Jews, too, when the Lord's spirit of religious liberty prevails in your midst.

Hanukkah, 5728

DON'T STAND OUTSIDE

Hanukkah is an assault on the profane.

I am speaking now about the term in its root meaning, and not in its extended and more conventional sense. Profane is from two Latin words—*pro*, which means "before" or "outside," and *fanum*, "temple." Outside the temple, that's the core meaning of profane. The word came to be used to describe the type of irreverent behavior and blasphemous language that could be heard only outside the temple, but never inside. I revert now to the basic meaning of the term.

For that, it seems to me, is so essentially involved in the significance of Hanukkah. The holiday was occasioned by the victory of the Maccabees who, as the traditional prayer spells it out, "came into the sanctuary of God's house," and, in so doing, got rid of the profane. The central episode of the Festival was the entering into the Temple. This is what Hanukkah is all about—the triumph which lies in overcoming the profanity of being on the outside. Come into the Temple, don't be an outsider—this is the thrust of the celebration.

Come inside. For one thing, we might think of that summons as it pertains to the fundamentals of living. Far too many of us remain outsiders, come the real stuff of human existence.

I came upon some disquieting statistics the other day. In the richest and most civilized country in the world, people spend infinitely more of their means on clothing accessories and jewelry than they do on religion and welfare. Two and a half times more is expended on drink than on medical care, three times more on tobacco than on private education and research. It inevitably raises my eyebrows when, from certain quarters, I am the recipient of assertions that "they can't afford the costs of Jewish education and synagogue participation." There is something obscene about our sense of

118

values when we remain outsiders and allocate more for the externalities of life than we do for the internals of our humanity. It's a profanity that is much more serious than the awful language you used last summer when your club failed to contact the golf ball.

Come inside. It's an invitation that many will do well to heed vis-à-vis the sanctuary of parenthood. It's a frightening thought, but factual and true nonetheless. Too many modern parents, for all their undeniable love for and generosity to their offspring, are only marginally involved with their children. I have a healthy appreciation for self-direction and self-expression, nor do I especially espouse the authoritarian approach. But this is a far cry from the kind of permissiveness, which is often really only a euphemism for estrangement and lack of concern, that is prevalent in contemporary parental attitudes. It is a profane scene to behold mothers and fathers who don't know their own children.

Come inside. I asked a member the other day whether the front doors of our synagogue opened in or out. He didn't remember. How should he? He hasn't walked in for the longest of times. It hurts me grievously when I contemplate the number of our people who, in the instance of the synagogue, are such blatant outsiders. In many ways, what goes on inside our institution is of the very vitality of Jewishness—worship, study and culture, identification, sociability. And yet, they are foreign to it all.

The chances are that, if you are reading this column, it's not meant for you. Do me, then, a favor. In this season of Hanukkah, tell the others that not only do Syrian-Greeks defile the Temple; tell them that Jews themselves profane their Sanctuary. Tell them to come inside.

Hanukkah, 5733

THE TRICK OF PURIM

I appreciate that it's not good form for a rabbi to sound a note of fatalism.

I shall be the first to admit that all too frequently we conjure up luck as an excuse and alibi. Someone once observed that, whether or not it's bad luck to meet a black cat depends on whether you are a man or a mouse. Max O'Rell had a point when he wrote, "Luck means the hardships and privations which you have not hesitated to endure, the long nights you have devoted to work." Amen. There is certainly time and place when that needs saying, there are certainly people for whom that is very relevant torah.

But for all our bravado, and perhaps wishful thinking, one cannot blithely dismiss the sway of circumstance, the accident of fortune, luck or fate or destiny, or whatever you call it. Walter Lippman described the dilemma of our time by saying: "For as long a time as we can see into the future we shall be living between war and peace, between a war that cannot be fought and a peace that cannot be achieved." What a hell of a no-man's land in which to be caught. It's not your doing, nor mine; but is there onyone who deludes himself in thinking that he can transcend this fateful placement?

Twenty-four hundred years ago our ancestors in the expansive empire of Persia, through no fault on their part, were caught in a fatefully tragic situation. How apt the name of the occasion. Purim, which literally means "lots." An irrevocable decree for their destruction went forth, and by *purim*, by lots, it was decided when they were to be decimated. Yet, and this is the glorious significance of the season, our ancestors turned Purim into a festival. Unable to have the decree revoked, they could, however, steel themselves against it and give it battle. In this manner did they turn fate into a festival.

Of course, in one way or another, we are all subject to fate. But our relief and deliverance lie in the fact that, while we live with the inevitable, we can arm ourselves against it and moderate its deleterious effects. Beer-Hoffman put it well, "The road is predestined, but the way we walk it, the attitude with which we bear our fate, can be of great influence over events." To acknowledge fate, and yet not be a fatalist; to be a realist, and yet not be a defeatist—that's the trick of Purim.

Tradition has it that, should all the other Festivals be abolished, Purim will remain. Here is a bit of unpopular realism that I share. For the foreseeable future Jews are fated to live in an essentially hostile and potentially anti-Semitic world. It's an unkind cut of destiny; but if we equip ourselves and face up to it, we can live with this reality and get the better of it.

You've been cheated in life? Who hasn't, in one way or another? Perhaps cheated out of some health, or some brains, or some beauty. We all have to live with some uninvited unpleasantness of one stripe or another. But the point is, life can only cheat you so much, and then you cheat yourself the most when you surrender. Cervantes once said: "A stout heart breaks bad luck." We Jews put it this way: Purim can be a *yomtov.*

Purim, 5726

WHAT MAKES HIM WISE?

Just because someone is clever doesn't necessarily mean that he is *ipso facto* a fine human being. Brilliance, as we can all attest from experience, doesn't automatically spell out goodness. We all know intellectuals who, as far as qualities of character are concerned, leave a great deal to be desired. All deference to the intellect, but the fact is there is no equating intellectuality with morality.

All of which creates a bit of an enigma when we come to the Haggadah passage dealing with the four sons. In that well known depiction of the four types, the wise son is contrasted with the wicked son. As if the opposite of an evil person is a clever individual, as if the counterpoise of wickedness is brilliance! Is there imbedded herein a strain of intellectual snobbery, the arrogant assumption that in order to be good you have to be a "brain"?

I hardly think so. I am persuaded that our confusion issues from a miscomprehension. When the Haggadah speaks of the "wise son," it doesn't necessarily mean a brilliant and erudite student, a member of the intellectual elite. He is called wise, not because he is brainy, but only because he exercises his mind. Put it this way —he's called a *hacham,* not because he's an intellectual, but only because he's intelligent.

The American writer Leo Stein observes that one of the marks of intelligence is open-mindedness. I recently heard an open mind defined as one that is too porous to hold a conviction. To be sure, there is that aspect about it. But having made allowances for that consideration, there is the other side of the coin to reckon with. King Solomon a long time ago counselled: "The beginning of wisdom is get wisdom." In this light, a *hacham* is not necessarily a person who has wisdom, he's rather a person who wants to get wisdom; he's not the learned one, he's the one who wants to learn; he's not the fellow who knows, he's the person who wants to know

122

—the person who opens his mind and genuinely seeks the truth so that he can be honest with himself and the world. Unquestionably, that's the moral and fair thing to do—to open your mind. And if many a mind is kept closed, it is for a variety of reasons. Perchance it's because of laziness; to open one's mind and think is strenuous. Perhaps it's because we don't like to be nagged by doubts. Writes Mr. Stein, "Some people are never in doubt; either they know nothing or they are sure; but often their ignorance is really their best guarantee." Lately, more and more note has been taken of what has been called our "barbarism of specialization." A distinguished philosopher laments the fact that today, when there are more scientists than ever, there are fewer cultured men than, for example, in 1750. We are too prone to close our minds to anything outside our particular interest. But clearly the most prevalent cause of closed minds is the human foible of prejudice, that trait which has been well described as "weighing the facts with your thumb on the scale."

Whatever the reason and cause, a closed mind is not only an intellectual failing, it's a moral delinquency. A person with a closed mind is an unfair person. The Haggadah is altogether in order—morality requires intelligence. You don't have to be an intellectual, but it's the essence of goodness to be intelligent and keep an open mind.

Pesach, 5726

ARE YOU ON ASKING TERMS WITH YOUR CHILDREN?

There is so much in the Passover Festival, especially in its unique ritual of the Seder, that is calculated to tickle the inquisitive bone of the young people and provoke their queries. Pesach has transmuted the conditional quality of the Scriptural "And it shall be if thy son asketh" into a positive imperative: make sure that your young people ask questions. Inquiry is one of man's finest proclivities, and Passover would have us encourage it in our children.

How? What does one do to create an ambience of inquiry and foster an asking-terms relationship with one's offspring?

The first and most obvious course is to provide in our schedule of existence something which is becoming rarer and rarer today, namely, an opportunity for conversation and discussion. The fact is that in today's busy world, our contacts, even within the bosom of the family, are so exiguous, our meetings so fleeting and shallow. We aren't together enough to provoke that give and take, that probing and questioning, those challenges and exchanges, which distil such wholesome results. To be on asking terms with our children, we need to create a more genuine pattern of family living.

It requires a setting, and it calls for this, too—we have to be the kind of people who can be asked. We have to be askable.

And some of us are not. Perhaps it's impatience that gets in our way. Basically we are doers and not talkers, and we simply haven't the time or endurance for mental calisthenics and discussions. Frequently, it's becaue we are not sure of ourselves and we don't want to incur an opening for our undoing. No one is so convinced as the unsure. We have a way of securing our shaky position with an impatience that permits no analysis. At times, it's a little more than impatience; at times, it's a type of temperament, a disposition, an authoritarian personality, a dogmatic individuality, that gets in the way. Whatever the cause, we are not always the askable folk we should be.

124

Above all, to strike an asking relationship with our children we have to be interesting people—people who stand for something, people who are committed to something, people who are involved in more than just the asinine and prosaic humdrum of human existence.

Beware of the trap of idealization, but it strikes me that yester-year was different with the adult world. There was an "ism" in its living. Visibly in the home parents stood for and carried out a program of Jewish living. Looking back, the struggle to make Palestine a Jewish country found a presence and reality in our midst. There was Zionism. During the depression years, willy-nilly we were more idealistically oriented and inclined in the direction of social issues and causes. The war years found us all ideologically engaged and concerned. But then the post-war years arrived; and in the glut of their affluence somehow we doffed every trace of spirituality and ideology, every semblance of involvement and commitment. To put it bluntly, we became, too many of us in the adult world, blah people. We are scarcely the kind of persons to provoke the interest and thinking of our young, we're not the kind of people worth asking.

Let Pesach do this much for us this year. Let it put us on asking terms with our children.

Pesach, 5729

THE RELUCTANCE TO GET OUR FEET WET

It takes trouble.

Anything worthwhile takes trouble. And very often the trouble is that we don't want to be troubled. A Yiddish apothegm picturesquely puts it this way: "The cat likes fish, but hates to wet her paws."

Our ancestors in Egypt indubitably longed for liberation and freedom from their bondage. But the reading of the Biblical tale clearly reveals that, for all their aspirations, they didn't exactly fancy what it took to achieve their emancipation. Threatened on the shores of the Red Sea by the pursuing Egyptians, they turned on their leaders with recriminations for positioning them between the devil and the deep blue sea. Of course they would have loved to attain the shores of freedom that lay beyond the water. *Ober vi kumt di kats iber di vasser?* "But how does the cat get across the water?" No, had it been left to our ancestors, had there been no Moses and Aaron, there would have been no Exodus. They didn't have the guts for the trouble it takes.

The trouble it takes.

Like the trouble that is inescapably entailed in the struggle for equality in our hemisphere. One detects more frequently nowadays the assailment of second thoughts amongst liberals vis-à-vis the whole course of the civil rights movement. The rise of the Negro's status has, in all truth, generated a great deal of disruption and bother in the comfortable existence of many a decent and well-intentioned individual. There is no getting away from it. The racial revolution, which we so devoutly espouse in theory, becomes troublesome when it impinges on our personal lives. Before it's done with, the reparation of old wrongs is going to take a lot of trouble.

"Whoever tries for great objects must suffer something," apho-

126

rized Plutarch a long time ago. That is ever the case. That's what some of us have been arguing for a long time now about Jewish religious life. Full religious freedom doesn't exist yet for the Jews in Israel, not because of the strength of the reactionary orthodox forces, but because of the diffidence of the liberals and secularists to get embroiled in a *kultur kampf*. Many a religious incongruity persists in our own community; only because, as someone euphemistically put it to me, we don't want any headaches and opt for letting things ride as they are. Changes are in the air in our own congregation. And there are many among us who, down deep, would like something along those lines but are afraid of stirring up any hornets' nests. There is the reluctance of getting our feet wet.

The trouble it takes. I wonder if with this phrase we haven't hit upon a basic cause for the poor results which our contemporary generation has had in the area of family life. It's an illusion to think that it was ever easy to rear children. If, however, somehow other generations seemed to have elicited better results, it's not because the children were better then. In large measure, it's because, unaccustomed to ease and not expecting to have things come easily, yesterday's parents weren't so sparing of themselves and took the trouble that is inextricably involved before one can taste the semblance of *nachas* from offspring. Marriage is not less successful today because it is more complicated. It always took trouble—a going marriage. But people today are less given to being bothered.

Everything worthwhile takes trouble. The whole point is that we have to be prepared to be troubled.

Pesach, 5732

TROUBLES ENOUGH OF MY OWN

The story is told of a merchant who came to Moses Sofer, the great Rabbi of Pressburg, and poured out his heart before him. He was in grave financial straits and begged now that the Rabbi, who was a renowned saint, give him his blessing. The Rabbi replied, "I have heard, sir, that your brother is very poor and in need, and that you do not help support him." "But Rabbi," apologized the merchant, "I have just told you how difficult my own position is. I have my own troubles; how can I help him?" Whereupon, Rabbi Sofer proceeded to read the man a lesson. "Scripture states that God said to Moses, 'And I also have heard the groaning of the Children of Israel whom the Egyptians keep in bondage.' What is the significance of the word 'also' in this text? It appears in the verse in order to teach us that, although every Israelite had his own woes and troubles under the oppressive bondage of the Egyptians, his own reason to sigh and groan, nonetheless every Israelite still heard the lamentation of his brother and was pained by his fellow's hurt. As a reward for this broader concern in a moment of personal travail, God 'also' heard their groaning and was moved to bring them salvation."

It is true, adversity often has a way of humanizing an individual. Difficult experiences do make us more understanding and sympathetic human beings. But sometimes, when hardship strikes, it can also have the opposite effect. Far from making us sensitive to the woes of others, at times it leads us to become so pre-occupied with our own problems that we actually grow impervious to the lot of those around us. Troubles enough of my own. This has a familiar ring, doesn't it? We've heard it many a time, and more than likely have voiced it ourselves. I have troubles enough of my own, can't be bothered by others.

I heard someone remark that trouble seems to defy the law of gravity—for it's easier to pick up than to drop. That pretty much describes our human situation. We all have our individual problems, at least our individual concerns, something or other that bothers us. And this is the test. How do we react when seized with a personal difficulty? Do we forget the world round about us, concentrating only on ourselves and our lot; or can we, for all our own troubles enough, still feel for others as well? It's so easy to become obsessed with one's own struggle and forget that he is not the only one in the same boat. "Even a poor man who himself subsists on charity should give charity." This is the import of Mar Zutra's remark—come trouble, and you're not the only one.

You're not the only one. Consider, for one thing, that an awareness of this truth can prove helpful and be a source of strength to us. "Misery loves company" is not exactly a noble philosophy, but at times it is most encouraging to appreciate that we are not alone. When we hear the sighs of others, we realize that we are not singled out for adversity, and we are kept from the distortions of cynicism and self-pity. Consider again, when we overcome the temptation of self-preoccupation, we create a source of succor and fortitude for others. It's not always a matter of material assistance; sometimes the moral support we lend is even of greater significance. A Jewish proverb has it that even in paradise it's not good to be alone. How much more so in an hour of adversity. "Shared trouble is half consolation" is the way one rabbi put it. We know this in our bones—"a trouble shared becomes a trouble halved." It's a healthy thing for all concerned, when faced with trouble, not to lose sight of the straits of others.

Those of us who are engaged in communal affairs will readily confirm the enhancement that would derive from a heightened mutuality. I am aware that the various organizations and institutions in our midst have their own burdens. It is only, however, when they transcend their self-preoccupation and become sensitive to the broader needs about them that a real spirit of community is distilled.

There is hardly an area in life that wouldn't benefit from this kind of heightened mutuality. Surely there is room for more of it in the family setting. "My wife talks to herself," complained a man. "So does mine," said his friend, "but she doesn't realize it. She thinks

I'm listening." Too often, this is the case at home—we are so seized with our own interests and problems that we have no ear for the concerns of even our nearest and dearest.

The Exodus eventuated and freedom dawned when the Israelite in Egypt, for all his own personal predicament, felt for his neighbor as well. Troubles enough of your own? To be sure, but certainly not so many that you can't feel for others as well.

Pesach, 5733

BECAUSE OF OUR MERITS

There ought to be a new prayer—not to supplant the old one, but to supplement it.

Twenty-five years of existence, in the face of overwhelming odds, confirms it. Announced on May 14, 1948, it has proved to be a viable birth. It is abundantly clear to us Jews and the world at large that the reborn Jewish State is a reality. And there ought to be a new prayer.

For centuries we Jews have been castigating ourselves. At *Musaf* time on every festival we raised our plaintive voices, and, in the hearing of our own people and in the hearing of the whole world, we blamed ourselves. *Umipne hataenu galinu meartzenu*, we cry. "Because of our sins we were exiled from our country and banished far from our land." It was our own doing, our own fault. To be sure, there were great historical forces abroad over which we had no control. Roman conquest and domination were the fact of the day. Yet essentially it was our own sinfulness that enmeshed us in the web and caused the destruction. It was paramountly the Jews themselves who brought on the terrible *galut*.

If it is true that Israel lost its homeland nearly two thousand years ago because of its own doing, then let us now proclaim another truth, perhaps even a more compelling truth—the return to Zion, the creation of a new State of Israel; it, too, is Israel's own doing. Two millennia ago, we were exiled because of our sins; today we were redeemed because of our merit. Henceforth *Umipne hataenu* should be complemented by a new prayer: *Umipne zechuyotenu shavnu el artzenu*, "Because of our merits have we returned to our land."

Our own doing. There is no braggadocio intended here. We are not so benightedly presumptuous as to think that we did it single-handedly. There were other forces at work. The impetus of a Bal-

131

four Declaration is not to be underestimated. The role of the United Nations in 1947 was a potent factor. The challenge of the Holocaust was an indispensable catalyst. We are indeed indebted to friendly powers, and above all to the Supreme Power, to God our sustainer throughout history.

Ours was not a solo achievement. But this realism should not blind us to the major part that we did play in this miraculous story. When it was futile to hope, Israel hoped. When it was vain to pray, Israel prayed. When it was folly to colonize, Israel colonized. When it was unwise to invest, Israel invested. When it was ridiculous to see kings and speak to presidents and diplomats, Israel was ridiculous. When it was demented to make sacrifices, Israel was tried and proved its mettle. There is no gainsaying the fact that twenty-five years ago there emerged a generation of Jews who, through their own merit, wrested a miracle from the stuff of history and established the Jewish State.

Twenty-five years ago. That makes ours a new generation. There is every evidence to believe that we shall be no less resplendent in our Jewish merit. No one knows better than we ourselves of the uncertainty that attends tomorrow's promise. We know this is not the time to relax. Someone once said, "For they can conquer who believe they can." We believed up to now, and we did conquer. We shall continue to believe, we shall continue to conquer, until we have brought peace and blessing to the new Jewish State. We mean to earn a new prayer—"Because of our merits we kept our land."

Iyar 5, 5733

THE TRAGEDY OF THE SIDELINES

It's an eerie lament which Arnold Weinstein sounds when he wails, "I lost touch. I lost such touch." To be around, and yet not be in touch with the stuff of life, that's the irony and the sadness of many an existence.

Says the Bible of our ancestors, as they witnessed the Revelation unfolding at Mount Sinai, that "they stood at a distance." Party to the most momentous event in history, and what did they do? They retired to the sidelines and left it all to Moses; they chose to be spectators instead of players in the great drama. What a pity, what a waste, this standing at a distance and being out of touch!

This detachment is a stance that is more characteristic of some periods than of others. It certainly is a palpable mark of our own time. Back in seventeenth century England, Ben Jonson could write, "Though the most be players, some must be spectators." Our contemporary Ben Jonsons would have to reverse that and say, "Though some be players, the most are spectators."

We fall out of touch, even in our inter-personal relationships. Sholem Aleichem once wryly said, "People love one another from a distance." Somehow or other, we allow our relationships to dwindle into marginal affairs. It is no accident that one would be hard put today to single out in contemporary literature or drama the one-time wonted themes of friendship and loyalty. It's safer to keep your distance and not become involved.

Has something of this aloofness infected the calibre of our family life as well? *Au courant* was the phrase he used in my study the other day. He was not *au courant*, he said, with his son's world. What he really meant was that he was out of touch with his son. This greater tolerance and leeway which we have introduced into our family living, and of which we are so proud, are

133

they really the products of understanding or rather the symptoms of detachment?

Dante once said that "the hottest places in hell are reserved for those who, in a period of moral crisis, maintain their neutrality." Neutral sidelines are comfortable for spectators but are hardly the benches for players. We're on the scene all right, but somehow far enough removed as not to be personally embroiled in the crucial social, political and economic affairs that are tormenting our times. We applaud Mr. Hochhuth's thesis that the world at large was guilty for not intervening in the Hitler madness. And then some of us turn around and act as if the great struggle of the colored people of the world for equality were not our business.

Marginal Jews come in all kinds of assortments. They are rampant in intellectual circles, where bright people analyze Judaism detachedly rather than live it intimately. They people the memberships of all kinds of Jewish organizations, where they belong without becoming involved. They cheer from the bleachers the renaissance of Hebrew culture and the rebirth of Israel, and yet are not flesh of the flesh of our emerging history.

There is in every time and every clime an episode of Sinai. What a waste, when we are witness to a revelation of God's hand in man's affairs, to stand at a distance and be out of touch with history in the making.

Shavuot, 5726

DON'T VICTIMIZE YOURSELF

Are you cheating yourself?

"Thou shalt not steal." In a more subtle and expanded sense, the thrust of the Eighth Commandment can be taken to mean: not only from your neighor, but not even from yourself.

How do we rob ourselves? In a variety of ways.

Consider, for example, the phenomenon of denying ourselves things that rightfully accrue to us. People, and sometimes whole groups of people, will go against the grain of their own disinctiveness in order not to be different. For the sake of conformity, they will deprive themselves of that individuality which is rightfully theirs. An unfulfilled potentiality is a kind of violence that an individual perpetrates against himself. It is, indeed, sad when circumstance prevents one from developing his intellectual capacities; how much more grievous, even sinful, when through sheer indolence and neglect of opportunities one cheats himself of the fruits of his faculties.

In a society that enjoys the freedom of faith, it is not but self-theft that accounts for the want of an elevating and satisfying religious experience. Ben Zoma, a Jewish sage of Talmudic days, was in wont of pausing and saying: "How much labor Adam must have expended before he obtained bread to eat, whereas I get up in the morning and find it prepared for me; and how much labor Adam must have invested before he obtained a garment to wear, whereas for me the artisans attend to my wants and I find all these things prepared for me." Do we, like Ben Zoma, take time out to reflect upon and appreciate the innumerable benefactions which cater to our needs; or do we, through indifference and callousness, rob ourselves of the ennobling and joyous spiritual experience of gratitude?

The Rabbis speak of "stealing the mind" of a person, by which

135

they mean the act of deception. In this light, consider how we rob ourselves when we indulge in self-deception.

Wishful thinking, the perversion of reality to accommodate a selfish desire, is naught but a self-deceptive indulgence. I have a great deal of respect for the ambitions which parents harbor for their children. More often than not they are woven of the fabric of love, wisdom and experience. But I must admit that there are parents who pathetically blind themselves to their children's abilities and would push them into pursuits not suitable for their powers. To fool oneself can engender a great deal of damage.

Vanity is so often but an unrealistic and exaggerated estimation of oneself, a baneful instance of self-delusion. It is a costly and impoverishing logic that implants the attitude "I'd rather not go at all if I can't go first class; I'd rather be no member than just a member; I'd rather not give at all if I can't give prominently. It's a kind of pride, and not sincerity, that keeps a man from being at least somewhat religious when he can't be completely faithful. Pride has a way of stunting our growth. It keeps us from making the most of our limited average selves and robs us of those benefits which are within our reach.

Caught cheating at his game of solitaire, the lunatic confessed that he had been cheating himself for years at the game. "Don't you ever catch yourself cheating yourself?" asked the amazed fellow inmate. "No," he replied proudly, "I'm too clever."

On this Festival of the Ten Commandments, I am asking that we be not "too clever." Thou shalt not steal—not even from yourself.

Shavuot, 5733

AND MY VOICE IS TO THE SONS OF MEN

Proverbs 8:4

PRINCIPLES ARE NOT ENOUGH

We are all familiar with, and decry it, too: the phenomenon of observing the letter and missing the spirit. There is something farcical and futile about concentrating on a detail and neglecting the essence. But it's the converse of this tack that prompts our comment in this piece.

All too often we have a way of observing the spirit and missing the letter, of deferring to the principle and ignoring the detail. Someone once said, "If we could make a great bonfire of the thousands of laws we have in this country, and start all over again only with the Ten Commandments, I am sure we would get along much better." I do not for one moment underestimate the importance of decisive principles, but I must differ most vehemently with the suggestion that they alone can suffice. For all their significance and indispensability, principles by themselves are not enough.

Principles without concern for details just won't do, because fundamentals of this kind usually prove to be vague and nebulous generalities that wield no real influence and effect no actual difference one way or another. More than that, principles without particulars, too, often become a reprehensible tool of alibi, procrastination, even of hypocrisy and evasion.

What's the phrase "in principle"? A request is made of us, and we're put on the spot. It's difficult for us to accede to the request, but to refuse would reflect very adversely on us. And so we do the political thing, we reply that "in principle" we agree but that we'll work out the particulars later. What a handy tool! At one and the same time, this "in principle" allows you to pass for a decent person while in practice, in the details that are the fare of concrete reality, you are something quite different. There is something patently empty and meaningless about principles which are not trans-

139

lated into specifics, about the "spirit of the thing" that is not incarnated in tangible deeds.

The minutes of a company board disclosed that all the directors were in sympathy with the employees' request for a raise in wages, but were not in favor of the hike. How easy it is, and what a balm to our conscience, to sympathize. To follow through on that sympathy, however, and to spell out its implications is a horse of a different color. Our life is studded with sympathies that, somehow or other, don't engender the favor of visible proof.

In the society of decent men today, no one will doubt that the principle of brotherhood is one to which all subscribe. In my circle, I know of no one who is not heart and soul for racial equality and does not espouse the principle of desegregation. Yet, some of my friends will forgive me if I aver that evidence of their idealism is not always palpable in the stuff of their personal conduct. When it comes to the proof of the pudding, when it's a matter of translating their beliefs into the changes, and sometimes sacrifices, in their own mode of life that are the logical consequences of their stance, there is a glaring show of diffidence.

I take it that "in principle" we are all for the survival of Judaism. The principle is there, and there's no aspersing it. But in too many cases, what is missing, woefully lacking, are the details of Jewish living that make up the entity of Judaism. There's no meaningful way of being with us in spirit save you express your Jewishness in concrete particulars.

All hail the man of principles, provided he spell them out in detail.

December, 1965

MITZVAH AND PUBLICITY DON'T MIX

We ought to make less noise—all of us, young and old alike—about our virtues.

"Formerly, a public man needed a private secretary for a barrier between himself and the public," writes Professor Daniel Boorstin, in his book *The Image*. "Nowadays he has a press secretary to keep him properly in the public eye." The professor is alluding, of course, to the publicity orientation of our times. In this publicity-obsessed age of ours, when everyone angles to catch the TV camera's eye and to make the headlines, the humble and retiring individual is hardly the paragon. We encourage people to "make the most" of their accomplishments and not to hide their achievements. The whole tenor of our society is inhospitable to the quiet and unostentatious, and invites instead the obtrusive qualities of boasting and boosting.

All of which reminds us of a lesson which Rabbi Levi Yitzchak conveyed to his followers. When a man commits a sin, said the saintly Rabbi, and knows he sinned, what does he do? He waxes contrite and repents his wrongdoing. But when a man performs a *mitzvah*, a good deed, and brags about it, this is not *mitzvah*, it in an *averah*, a sin. Perhaps sin is too harsh a term. We are, however, familiar with the phenomenon, and perchance we can label it "obtrusive goodness"—you know, all those great things we do with so much noise and broadcast. Rabbi Levi Yitzchak is entering a plea for unobtrusive goodness, for virtue without braggadocio.

Why? I suppose, for any number of reasons. To begin with, there's the matter whereof Dr. Louis Finkelstein writes in his book *The Pharisees*. "Humility," he observes, "comes only with maturity." There is something obnoxiously infantile about the need for applause and recognition for every accomplishment. Vaunting chafes us with its immaturity, irritates us with its stridency.

141

More damaging than that, the demonstrative *mitzvah* generates an ambience of insincerity. Inescapably, it begets the feeling that what is done is effectuated, not for its own sake, but for the sake of projecting an image. It's a sobering definition—a hypocrite is described as a man who sets good examples when he has an audience. There is an unavoidably false and disingenuous ring about our advertised goodness.

But perhaps its most serious fault is that it asperses the tone of our society at large. When virtue merits to be publicized, it would suggest that virtue is exceptional and that the standard is less than virtuous. When marital fidelity is something to brag about, it doesn't speak too highly of the prevailing tone of morality in our society. When honesty is something for us to prate about, we are virtually allowing that something less than honest is legitimate fare for the average.

Whatever the reasons, Rabbi Levi Yitzchak's plea is that we be unobtrusive in our achievements. Hats off to our intellectuals; but gifted people who consciously set themselves up as an intellectual elite have no call upon our approbation. It's one thing to be charitable; but quite another thing, and in no wise meritorious, to parade as a philanthropist. Religious faith and practice are no mean feats in these times, yet no one can blame us if we look askance at a piety that is loud and brassy. It's stirring to behold the idealism wherewith people will champion a cause, but somehow the crusade is tarnished when it postures and needs the theatric and spectacular.

Somehow *mitzvah* and publicity don't go together.

May, 1969

NEVER MIND THE SCORE

It's the results that count.

There's no gainsaying the importance of results; but having acknowledged this, there's more to the story. We can't espouse the philosophy wherein the consideration of results should be the determining factor of all our behavior.

A wife was late in meeting her husband at the ball game. She arrived during the fifth inning. "What's the score, dear?" she asked, out of breath. "Nothing to nothing," was his reply. "Oh, good," she exclaimed. "Then I haven't missed a thing."

It isn't always the score that determines the quality of the game. We've all witnessed games in which some of the most exciting and most commendable playing did not necessarily chalk up a winning goal. It's no different in the game of life. People can and do shine not only by the points they score, but even more so by the fight they put up, by the spunk and endeavor with which they invest their living. It isn't always important to win, but it is always important to battle for the right goal, regardless of the results.

Besides, isn't it true that very often we entertain a short-sighted view of results. We think of them in terms of immediate and tangible consequences, and tend to overlook the accumulative effect of our behavior. Any number of plays can go scoreless, but, in the end, it is precisely these very plays that can add up to a telling goal. The truth of the matter is, there is nothing that we do that is without results. We don't always have to win at the moment to get results.

In fact, we abdicate our responsibility and verge on the immoral when we condition our behavior on the expectation of results. And this is happening all the time. We see it when a community organization refuses to adopt a position on the grounds that such a stand has no chance of winning at this juncture. One wonders

143

what progress society could have made if our idealists had always thought in terms of the practicality of results. It's not always important to be successful, but it is important to be right.

"What's the use of my telling him?" complained a mother about her son. "He won't listen to me." It's increasingly hard these days to get results from our teenagers, and so many of us don't even try any more. Immorally, we short-change our parental duty when we restrict our guidance merely to the acceptable. It's not always important that you win with your child, but it is important for you to put up a fight and let him know where you stand. Besides, who knows, nag and fight long enough, play your best, and ultimately you may score.

October, 1964

CARE IF YOU CAN'T CURE

Some time ago, John Foster Dulles was reported in a national magazine as saying, "The measure of success is not whether you have a tough problem to deal with, but whether it's the same problem you had last year." There's no gainsaying the sense of frustration and futility bred by the insoluble. When we work, we want results. It's not that we necessarily insist on material reward; it's just that we do not regard ourselves as successful unless our efforts manifest progress and achievement. We want to get somewhere with our labors.

But there lurks a danger in this human inclination of ours. Unfortunately, not all problems with which we are confronted are soluble. There are situations in life with which we can't do very much and which do not allow us to score the achievement we would like. Our potentialities may be there, but the particular challenge with which we are seized does not always permit us to exercise them to the full. Very often, in such instances, our drive for success prompts us to abandon the unrewarding and to concentrate on that which is more promising. Yet, what about the irremediable and not so promsing? Does our aspiration for success so insensitize and brutalize us that we doom them to an existence of neglect and indifference?

There's an individual who's been haunting my study for a long time now. She's a pathetic figure and I really can't help her in her problems. I am sometimes tempted to sever her visits once and for all and devote the time she takes from me to more fruitful advantage. But then, I am overcome by an awareness that mine is not always to cure, but sometimes, only to care.

It was along these lines that our discussion at the welfare agency veered. The suggestion was made that more could be achieved by our social workers if the "hard core" cases were eliminated, or at

145

least relegated to the background, and more time devoted to those who can be rehabilitated. It would, indeed, be a waste if everything possible were not done with those who can be helped. They deserve our best and most skilled effort. But can we in any way be justified in depriving the "hard core" of our solicitous concern and attention? Surely the achievement of a social service agency calls for more than just successful case loads.

I intend no stricture against the psychiatric profession as such. Yet, one gets the impression, from my vantage, that some practitioners of this field of medicine are too apt to devote their time to problematic situations rather than to instances of real mental illness. Is it, perchance, because they want concrete results and balk at the frustration of dealing with what is so often the hopeless? I understand that therapy is the physician's primary role, but even when he can't succeed in healing, there is still call for his ministrations.

All credit to the recent developments which have pioneered in the rehabilitation of the chronically ill. Many, who heretofore were considered as beyond help, are today the recipients and beneficiaries of restorative treatment. This does not hide the fact, however, that we still have with us the incurable for whom no treatment will avail. And for these, the hard core, it seems to be getting more difficult to find proper care and attention. To be sure, it is dreadfully disheartening to be involved in work that can issue in no dramatic betterment and offers no possibility of a success story. But because we are human beings, we must help even if we can't cure.

Years ago, Martin Buber wrote: "We Jews, we of the blood of Amos and Jeremiah and Spinoza and all the earth-shatterers who died unsuccessful, we know a different world history from this one which subscribes to success."

January, 1965

COMMUNICATING WITHOUT SELLING

It is passing strange that advertising, which has doubtlessly done so much to enhance the art of communication in our society, has at the same time done no little to stymie it and invest it with obstacles. And because communication lies at the root of all our interpersonal relationships, in one way or another we are all affected. In a very real sense, advertising has made it very difficult to communicate.

For one thing, the very surfeit of advertising and constant selling to which we are exposed every waking hour of the day have insinuated in us a kind of "non-listenability." It's almost a necessary defense mechanism. It would simply be intolerable if we had to take cognizance of all that aims to catch our attention. We ward it off, as it were, by developing the habit to ignore. We can look without seeing, we can listen without hearing. Hence the repetitiveness in advertising, even nagging. The calculation is that if you stay at it long enough, finally you'll get through.

But even when the break-through is made, our guard is still up. This is the second result of the self-defeating aspects of advertising. We simply don't believe what we're told. And with good reason. Jules Henry, in his recent book *Culture Against Man*, has a chapter on advertising as a philosophical system. Surveying the palpable exaggerations and ridiculous claims that infest the sales pitch, he speaks of "a new kind of truth that has emerged which may be defined as a false statement made as if it were true, but not intended to be believed." In the same vein, one of the characters in Charles Yost's recent book of dialogues inveighs against us that "the most subversive of your techniques is advertising which seems designed to build up in the community a tolerance of insincerity by repeating shamelessly over and over claims which everyone knows to be false." In fine, advertising tends to make us cyni-

147

cal and breeds in us the habit to disbelieve. Even when we hear, we take it only as a "line."

Habituated as we are in this age of advertising to ignore and disbelieve, it's increasingly difficult to get through to people in any area of communication. Modern parents know this only too well. Too often it's a sheer struggle and takes no little nagging before they can even communicate their point to their children. And then, more often than not, it's not taken seriously, for after all "it's only the usual parental line."

Those who are engaged in communal endeavors and causes know the frustration of this phenomenon. Though there is nothing commercial in their aims, frequently they are compelled to resort to a Madison Avenue approach to convey their objective and elicit a response. I can buy for the nonce the counsel that you have to spend money to make money. Yet, when it's not money that we're after, when it is rather an objective of a higher and nobler nature, it seems a shame to have to mount a campaign and waste so much effort and means to get any results.

If all this sounds as if I'm giving air to a peeve, you're absolutely right. Nothing is more piquing to a rabbi than the fact that all too often he has to "sell his wares." To break the barrier of their indifference and cynicism, to communicate with his people, he is obliged to spend needless time and effort, hammering away and persuading. As if religion were a piece with a detergent that it needs a pitch to be put across. As if a rabbi preaches what he does because that's his line.

Life is more than a commercial venture, and not everything is business. We should be able to communicate without having to sell.

January, 1965

THE PRICE OF "NEWLATRY"

Back in 1835, there appeared an editorial which warned that "Railroads, if they succeed, will give an unnatural impetus to society, destroy all the relations which exist between man and man, overthrow all mercantile regulations, and create, at the peril of life, all sorts of confusion and distress." The prospect of the new has always generated anxiety in some of us. There is a natural propensity to suspect change and fear its consequences. There's no doubting that, were we to surrender to this timidity and gingerly approach to life, we should soon strangle all progress and wallow in stagnation. The status quo rarely represents the best of all possible realities; there is always room for the new.

Having said that, however, we are prompted to sound a note of caution. There is abroad today a kind of worship of the new which is intemperate in its fervor and blind in its insistence. On the contemporary scene, our erstwhile pursuit of happiness has been replaced by the pursuit of status. And as Dr. Louis Kronenberger astutely observes in one of his essays, "The basis of every status symbol is that it must asperse the status quo. . . . Wherever the standard of living enters in, the past, even the immediate past, is simply a slum." In our drive for status-conferring newness and difference, we've come to disparage the old and disdain the familiar.

It's a costly and unfortunate development, for in effect this worship of the new can deprive us of some of the most stabilizing influences in our lives. For one thing, it has all but eliminated contentment from our scheme of things. In constant desire for the novel, we lack the steadying experience of finding satisfaction in what we have. With our wants always and ever irritated, we hardly know any more what it means to be pleased. What does the Yiddish call it—"climbing the walls." We are fast losing the capacity simply to enjoy life.

149

It robs us, too, this idolization of the new, of the sustaining fruits of loyalty. Our bonds with people are loosened and our relationships become tenuous and fleeting. Our continuous aspiring for new contacts and different circles of acquaintance too easily engenders neglect of former ties and associations. Gone are the firmer aspects of human fellowship. We no longer have friends, only people that we meet and rub elbows with for a while.

It goes without saying that our passion for the new has all but obliterated the concept of tradition. When change becomes an end in itself, nothing can last long enough to become sacred. Haven't we hit here upon one of the root causes of the sense of drift which prevails in our midst? We are bereft of those mores and traditions that furnish the guide-lines of living.

The adulation of the different tends in some to sever every kind of meaningful attachment. Yesterday's espoused ideals dissipate before more stylish causes. Indeed, we seem to operate less by values and convictions than by fads and vogues. Unrooted in principles, we become a crowd of enthusiasts with superficial dedications. We have few real attachments, only new binges and kicks.

Let no one misunderstand the above. We are not advocating stodginess. It's just that in our forward look we ought not lose sight of such stabilizing assets of life as contentment, loyalty, tradition and principle. Hail the new, but yesterday and today have something to offer as well.

February, 1965

WILL OUR CHILDREN FORGIVE US?

It was a revealing session, and no little disconcerting, too. The young man had good reason to be in my study; to say the least, he had made a mess of things. And now he was blaming his parents. He was bitter, not because they had not been devoted to him or had stinted in any way in their love and solicitude; but, as he put it, they had done him no favors. His acerbity here reminded me of that sardonic observation: "Children begin by loving their parents. As they grow older, they judge them. Sometimes they forgive them."

It's ironic that, for all our good intentions, sometimes we really don't do our children any favors. This is certainly true, as everyone recognizes, when we over-indulge them. We mean so well and there is no doubting our motivation. We want them to have everything, and especially those things that we missed out on. I hold no brief for unwarranted niggardliness with the young, nor do I espouse the philosophy of "let him come up the hard way as I did." But there is much point to Samuel Clarke's comment that "It is most important for our young men, as it is for our nation, that they be taught in their homes from their early youth that a man has work to do; that one who merely seeks his own pleasure proves himself unworthy of a place in the world. Our rapidly increasing wealth and unwise parental love are leading to many weak, worthless lives." The favors we do our children can eventuate in perverting their values and in depriving them of the initiative that is so necessary in the hurly-burly of adult life.

It's the rare parent who wants to hurt his child. But it's the common parent who makes excuses and weaves alibis for his offspring's weaknesses and failings. We cover up, we explain away, we make light of, we consciously overlook—we choose to view the foible as a passing phase. Even in his day, Rabbi Jose ben Hanina

151

had cause to remark in the Midrash, "Love without criticism is not love." The Sage well appreciated that it's a false favor we do our children when, in according them uncritical love, we rationalize away their faults. In the long run, this course is bound to be deleterious, for sooner or later an individual has to face the consequences of his real person and behavior.

I'm all for giving our children an extra push. Some don't need it, but there are undoubtedly others who need the bolstering and goading of their parents. The danger is, however, that we can overdo it. We see it all the time in our school. A mother will move heaven and earth to keep her child from the stigma of repeating the year, in spite of the fact that later successful academic work dictates a sound grounding now. Guidance and counsel are always in order and, more often than not, adult experience stands in good stead. Yet, there is the unhealthy phenomenon of the over-ambitious parent who is more propelled by his own pride and frustrations than by his child's capacities and needs.

It isn't always our fault. Young people have a knack all of their own of fouling up their lives. But I understood the plaint of the fellow in my office. Sometimes we're really not doing our children any favors; on the contrary, we help them make a mess of things.

January, 1966

GENEROUS FOR THE WRONG THINGS

Someone pointed out that the Scriptural story of the fashioning of the Golden Calf bespeaks the fact that man has worshipped wealth since time immemorial. The Jewish Sages say that there isn't a generation in human history that doesn't partake, in some measure or other, of the sin of the Golden Calf. But was that transgression of our ancestors in the wilderness some three thousand years ago really the foible of worshipping gold? *Au contraire*, had they been so enamored of wealth and riches, then surely, in all logic, they wouldn't have been so generous in contributing their gold for the fabrication of the idol. No, making an idol of gold was not their offense; their sin was that they used their wealth for the wrong thing.

And this, I suggest, is the tinge of that ancient sin in our own contemporary society. Joseph Wood Krutch, in one of his more recent books, points out that we are not materialists in the sense that we love wealth for its own sake. We are not misers, he declares; on the contrary, we are spendthrifts. We lavish away our riches on ourselves and others. Like that generation in the wilderness more than three millennia ago who squandered away their wealth on an idol, we, too, lavishly and generously, misuse our assets. This is our folly—of our riches we make but a monstrous calf. We're generous for the wrong things.

Take this a step further. Our wealth consists not only of material things, but is comprised of varied assets. In this broad sense, we enjoy the riches of emotion. Whatever else we are, we are not a cold, indifferent, unresponsive kind of people. To put it more positively, we are a people with lively feelings and emotions. We don't hoard our sentiments, we're generous with our feelings, we spend our emotions. But ofttimes we indulge them foolishly and for the wrong things.

I dare say, for example, that we are wont to spend more on hate

153

than on love. It's cynical but true! "Some people do odd things to get even." Charles Colton was a realist when he said that revenge is a much stronger principle than gratitude. We're not a bland and apathetic folk, we're not stingy with our feelings; we're sensitive and are ever ready to applaud the celebrated figure in our midst. We're generous with our commendation and liberal with our adulation. More often than not, however, the calibre of our hero on whom we shower our sentiments is so disappointing. I am sure no Nobel Prize winner nor any artist of distinction has ever received the kind of enthusiastic reception accorded the Beatles. James Reston makes the point when he writes that Americans need real heroes whom they can worship, not just nobodies inflated into celebrities by public relations machines.

What a shame to waste the riches of our talents and abilities on inanities. Professor Galbraith loudly bemoans the fact that so much of our research effort is devoted, in our affluent society, only to discovering changes that can be advertised. Too often the research program is built around the need to devise "selling points" or to accelerate "planned obsolescence." Make no mistake about it, the dearth of good literature and drama today is due to no paucity of creative talent, but to the misuse of that talent for market purposes. What a heartbreak, with all our talent we only fashion inanities.

Lazy? I sometimes think we are, but then again I am sure that most of us are basically industrious individuals, and even ambitious. We really do try. But, perchance, we try for the wrong things. Are we misusing our asset of industriousness? Frank Romer pungently points out, "The time men spend in trying to impress others they could spend in doing the things by which others would be impressed." Too much effort nowadays is expended on the creation of an image and not nearly enough on the real thing. Isn't it a misuse of our energies when we work to impress instead of labor to achieve?

We human beings are rich in so many different ways; and the sad fact is that, all too often, we don't worship our wealth, we spoil it.

March, 1966

DEMOCRACY WITHOUT RANCOR

Hate is one of the most dangerous and deleterious of our emotions. Admitted into the complex of our feelings, it's hard to get rid of. "The terrible thing about hatred," writes Valentin, "is that he who is seized with it as a rule does not wish to get rid of it." I am reminded of the misogynist who confessed, "I hate women and I am glad that I hate them; because if I didn't hate them, I'd like them, and I hate them."

There is this danger, too—hate grows to such proportions in us that it beclouds our thinking and vision. It degrades our dignity, disfigures our personality and character, undermines our health and eats away at our well-being. It can even derange us. It not only wreaks destruction on those round about its bearer, but it destroys the hater himself.

And there is a painful irony involved here. All too frequently, the more democratic our setting, the more conducive it is to the distillation of hatreds and hostilities. In a free and equal society, we are at a greater liberty to disagree with one another, to disapprove of one another; and lamentably, we haven't yet mastered the ability to disagree without disliking, to differ without being hostile, to disapprove without rancor and resentment.

I wonder if this observation doesn't go a way in explaining the apparent increase in family discord today. There is no denying that the democratization of the home has facilitated a greater expression of independence and divergence of thought on the part of its individual members. Husband and wife, parents and children feel freer to disagree with one another and often even hold opposing views. And because, by and large, we have not yet learned to differ without quarreling, our familial freedom is very apt to beget animus and hostility.

Jonathan Swift once said, "We have just enough religion to make us hate, but not enough to make us love one another." Perhaps nowhere does mutual disagreement incur more enmity than in the area of religion. As in all other areas of life today, there is a greater freedom in the ambit of faith, too, for individual interpretation and diversity. It is wholly understandable that there is little room in our democratic milieu for monolithic religious belief and practise. By the same token, this religious diversity of ours all too often breeds in us bellicose emotions and acrimonious hatreds. To say the least, the lack of mutuality between the three religious wings in Judaism is a regrettable and costly reality of contemporary Jewish life. No one is asking here for the surrender of conviction, but rather only for the spirit of the Rabbi from Stratin. Approached for a *segulah*, a charm, to ensure a greater love of God, the Rabbi answered: "Go and charm yourself, accustom yourself to love your fellow Jew; for there is no better charm for the love of God than the love of fellow man."

The great boon of liberty is our right to disagree. Concomitantly, the great challenge of liberty is to differ without rancor and hostility.

November, 1966

THE PITFALLS OF STUDENT POWER

A new underdog has been uncovered, and a clamor has gone up for his relief.

Our eyes have been opened of late to the deprivations of the university student. His struggle may assume various forms on the different campuses, but, beneath all the tumult, the basic issue is clear. Students have no say in the management and administration of the university and are denied the right to participate in the formulation of policy. And now there is a waxing effort to redress this wrong and effectuate a greater equality. There is abroad a very palpable struggle for student power.

All wisdom does not lie with age. An honest appraisal of the situation will, irrefragably, confirm the legitimacy of many of the specific gripes of the students. It would be fatuous to labor under the premise that Academe can do no wrong, that all is paradisiacal within its gates. There is room and room for improvement and betterment. But having allowed that, I somehow still find myself unsympathetic to the drive for student power. I would not want to see students participate in the administration of a university. And this for a congeries of reasons.

For one thing, I am persuaded that the process of educating young people requires an institutional context wherein there reigns a clear demarcation between the teachers and the learners. The fact is that they are not equals; and save there be an unmistakable deference on the part of the tutees for those who govern their program, the whole process of a meaningful and achieving education will disintegrate. One is reminded here of the acute pertinence of Rabbi Eleazar's admonition: "Let the reverence for your teacher be like the fear of heaven."

Secondly, for all their acknowledged brilliance, students are not yet quite competent and qualified to assume governing roles. If

157

nothing else, they lack the experience and especially the perspective that derive only from a maturity of years. The very exuberance of their youthfulness and the passion of their age deny them the judiciousness and sense of responsibility that must be the signature of university authority.

Thirdly, the short duration of the student's association with the university does not warrant his right to shape policy which will effect the institution long after he has made his exit from the scene. Very frankly, a student's interest is a vested and myopic stripe of interest. He will be gone, but the administration will have to be around to live with the consequences of his whims and fancies. It's simply unfair, in view of the student's tenuous and temporary investment, to make him part of management.

And finally, for me this is the most puissant argument against student power—it will necessarily undermine the greatest asset of the modern Western university: the academic freedom of its faculty. How diabolic! To give students power is necessarily to put professors at the mercy of their tutees. Nothing is more calculated to destroy the independence and freedom of college teaching than such an unfortunate arrangement. Paradoxically, in gaining power, students would only thwart their own best interests at the university; they would deny themselves the opportunity of pursuing an education in an institution that is blessed with academic freedom.

By all means, let there be better communication between students and university authorities. But let students remain students; and authorities, authorities.

December, 1967

IT TAKES MORE THAN KNOW-HOW

I hope it's more than know-how that characterizes the achievement of our graduates.

A New York socialite once came into the salon of Walter Florelle, the celebrated milliner, for a party hat. The craftsman took a couple of yards of ribbon, twisted it around, put it on her head and said, "There is your hat, madam." "It's magnificent!" exclaimed the woman. "Seventy-five dollars," said Walter. The customer was shocked and protested. "That much for a couple of yards of ribbon?!" Florelle unwound the ribbon and handed it to her saying, "For the ribbon? The ribbon, madam, is free."

Hats off to skill—or should we say here, hats on to skill. There is no gainsaying the crucial difference that skill makes in our scheme of things. Having acknowledged that, however, we are propelled to sound a caveat. Let's not make too much of it. For all the premium that our society puts on it, it takes more than know-how.

A long time ago, Aristotle noted that it is not sufficient to know what one ought to say, but how to say it. No one will cavil with this truth. How to say it, how to behave, how to give, how to get along with people—the skills of social behavior are not to be underestimated. But for all that, interpersonal relationships require more than just techniques. Far too often we lean too heavily on social graces and personality, and not nearly enough on genuineness and character. One doesn't have to espouse hippyism to realize that manners per se are only skin deep. It takes more than skill to be a member of human society. Above and beyond the pleasing externals of successful public relations, we need the substantial fare of such things as integrity and morality, of kindness and compassion.

In his book *Out of My Later Years*, Albert Einstein observes,

159

"Perfection of means and confusion of goals seem to characterize our age." The field of pedagogy is an especially vulnerable victim here, because it places so much emphasis on techniques and so little on content. I do not imply that know-how in teaching is unimportant. Obviously, it is very important and on certain levels even essential and indispensable. But, surely, here is one area where it takes more than just skill. It is not sufficient to know how to teach; one must have something to teach. Whatever else is needed to tone up our educational system, we need teachers who are proficient and even expert in their subject material. Forgive me if I am a heretic and advocate for our teachers—less psychology and more knowledge.

From campus quarters today come loud complaints about the irrelevance of college education. If the grievance alludes to an absence of concern for and a lack of relationship to the great moral issues of our time, if the dissatisfaction is with learning that is devoid of all ethical fibre, that's one thing. If, however, irrelevance refers to the *tachlis* and applicability that are missing in college fare, that's quite another thing. Certainly it is the task of a university to equip young people with professional skills and productive know-how. Yet, surely, a college education should be more than vocational-deep. It is something other than sheer practicality that characterizes the really cultured individual.

There is more to life than method. I hope that our graduates have gotten more than just know-how out of their academic pursuit.

June, 1968

THE MASQUERADE OF WORDS

Words don't always mean what they say.

I'm not sure that it's a form of hypocrisy, but to me it smacks very much of dissemblance and disingenuousness. I am well aware of the discretion which prompts us at times to euphemize, even the desirability of opting for mild and polite expressions to avoid giving offense and pain. At the moment, however, our allusion is to something distinctly less considerate and noble. Our focus is on innocent-sounding phrases that are employed to conceal something not so innocent. Basically, it's a dishonest indulgence, a misuse of language. Essentially, it's an act of dissimulation, if not outright hypocrisy. Words don't always mean what they say, because we don't always say what we mean.

The reader can indubitably call to mind any number of examples of this phenomenon. Perhaps, however, he will share with me a pique occasioned by three especially prevalent words of our milieu.

Communication. This is a very important word, for the whole social context depends upon the ability of individuals to convey to one another their thoughts and feelings. We are, indeed, in a sad state of affairs when we suffer a breakdown of communication. And to hear some of us tell it, that is precisely the dolorous condition in crucial areas of our relationships. Young people inform us that they cannot communicate with their parents. Students on the campus complain that they cannot communicate with faculty and administration. Congregants are bitter because they cannot communicate with their rabbi.

That's too bad. This is not said cynically. The lines should at all times be open, and it is regretful when they are not. The fact of the matter is, however, that we often carp that we can't communicate in spite of the fact that we are getting through. What we really mean is, not that the party doesn't hear us or understand us, but rather that the party is unwilling to accede to our way of thinking and refuses to obey us. We talk *communication* and mean having our way.

Relevance. We are probably more hung up on this term than on any other word in our times. Certainly there is justice in given situations for the demand for pertinence. Willy-nilly, life calls for its measure of practicality, and there are issues that we cannot avoid.

Forgive me, however, if frequently nowadays I distrust the cry of irrelevance. Someone told me the other day that the traditional code of morality is irrelevant for our society. Does he really mean that it is not relevant, that it has nothing to say about the conduct of our society? Or does he mean, rather, that while it has a great deal to say, he doesn't like what it has to say and won't buy it? We cry *irrelevance* and really mean that we object.

Confrontation. This is a loaded term and charged with ethical overtones. People of integrity should always be up to facing a matter squarely. There is no denying the immorality of evasiveness. Confrontation is the duty of each and every one of us.

I get the impression, however, that in too many quarters confrontation is a front term for unreasonable subjectivism, for intolerance, and more especially for violence and even attack. We piously invoke *confrontation* and we mean disruption and destruction.

Words don't always mean what they say, because ofttimes we are somewhat dishonest and don't say what we mean.

January, 1969

OBSCENE SPEECH

You are not necessarily a prude when you refuse to be crude.

Anyone who is at all familiar with the Bible knows that Scriptural literature is in no wise squeamish; nor is its subject material marked by an exaggerated modesty. If anything, the Bible is an altogether candid and straightforward book. Yet, for all its realism, it is never immodest or vulgar.

The case is much the same, and perhaps even more so, in the instance of our vast Rabbinic Literature. It never shies away from the most delicate of matters; nonetheless, it always manages to resist coarseness and makes it a point to couch its asseverations in a medium of refinement.

Jewish tradition is far from prudish; it has no tolerance, however, for profanity and obscene speech. Never utter an ugly word, admonish the Sages, and let a man make sure that he communicates with a clean tongue. Bothered by smutty expression, the Rabbis in the Talmud assert: "Whoever uses obscene language, even if a favorable decree of seventy years be to his credit, it will be altered to an unfavorable one. For him who uses obscene language, *gehinnom* (hell) is deepened; and this applies even to one who listens to such talk without protesting."

In many quarters today, this must sound like very irrelevant stuff. But to a square like me a tradition that discountenances our contemporary vulgarization of language sounds altogether pertinent and vital.

It's not only our lapsing into profanty, which at times, I suppose, is unavoidable if not inexcusable. I am talking now about the whole tenor of crudity and vulgarity in language which is becoming the vogue, and usually in more sophisticated and intellectual circles. The battle for free speech on the campus is all too often little more than a fight for the right to indulge in obscene speech. It has be-

163

come smart and modish to be uninhibited and express oneself in the earthiest of fashions. In many circles today, the fifty-cent word is a four-letter word.

And make no mistake about it—ours now is not just a goody-goody stance. Eric Partridge, the distinguished British etymologist and lexicographer, recently had cause to write in a magazine article: "Anyone believing in the worth and value of the human race . . . finds it difficult to condone, impossible to approve, and unthinkable to abet the most insidious and surest means of destroying civilization. To degrade language is to degrade civilization."

Mr. Partridge knows it in his bones, as it is, indeed, the healthy intuition of our own Tradition, that speech is more than just an act of expression. Language is influential and activative. Language is determinative. Language colors the character of a milieu, sets the tone of relationships. Foul language is more than just a release of foul feeling; inevitably, it generates and begets a foul ambience. How you talk decides how you, and even others, act. Coarse words sire coarse behavior; profanity, a profane demeanor. Obscene speech breeds obscene indulgences. A lewd tongue encourages lasciviousness and nurtures immorality. Dirty talk invites dirty deeds. Somewhere in the brewing of our violent society is the ingredient of violated language.

Language is a stimulant, a powerful catalyst. That is why we must be circumspect in its usage. You don't have to be a prude—only don't be crude.

January, 1969

MAKING IT THE WAY IT IS

Tell it the way it is.

That is the inviolable injunction of our times. It has such an utterly unhypocritical and honest ring about it. In the novel, on the stage, on television—tell it the way it is.

Let the brickbats fly, but I am not so sure that I can accept this unreserved candor as a categorical guideline. And this is for a number of reasons.

For the reason, to begin with, that I cannot buy the philosophy that truth alone is sanction enough for its communication. Tell it the way it is—without consideration of the after effects, without reckoning about to whom you tell it, how you tell it, when you tell it? No virtue is unqualifiedly a virtue. Maturity knows that even truthfulness has to be handled with *sechel*, which is a combination of sense and sensitivity. Save you be callous and inhumane, there are instances when you don't tell it the way it is.

For the reason, again, that it's *hutzpah* to act as if you indisputably know the way it really is, as if you had a monopoly on the truth. Says that homespun philosopher Mendele Mocher Seforim, in his story *Dos Kleine Mentshele:* "Truth is a word which each one understands in his own way, according to his own needs, as it suits him." One needs a little more humility. One needs to appreciate that what we generally hold to be true is largely a conclusion of what we interpret—not know, but interpret and feel and believe —to be the truth. In other words, it's our version of things—not necessarily the way it is, but the way we see it. There is a galling arrogance and presumption in purporting to present it the way it really is.

Moreover, more often than not, this is not a telling; it is, rather, an enacting. This is not reporting, it's indulging.

Some weeks ago, on a talk program over a New York City radio

165

station, a poem attributed to a fifteen-year-old black schoolboy was read by a black teacher. The piece was dedicated to the head of the Teacher's Union, and it began: "Hey, Jew boy, with that yarmulka on your head, You pale-faced Jew boy. I wish you were dead." When complaints were lodged with the host of the program, he said he appreciated the anti-Semitism involved, but that he was merely presenting realities as they were, he was merely relating the facts of life in New York.

I am not for sweeping controversial issues under the carpet. But I am contending that there is a vast difference between talking about black anti-Semitism on a program and enacting that malady. The first is an intellectual discussion, the second is an act of participation. You're not telling it, you're part of it.

Finally, "telling it the way it is" is frequently a disingenuous phrase. It would be more accurate to say "making it the way it is." Media not only reflect a situation: they do far more, they create and spread it. By virtue of their influence, they are catalytic and shape the realism they purport to mirror.

The rash of contemporary films, plays, and novels which profess to portray the immoralities and sexual aberrations of our society really do not so much describe as they encourage, abet and provide the stuff of our decadence. They are no innocent, objective depictions; they aren't telling it the way it is—they are making it the way it is.

Tell it the way it is. Are you reporting, or are you propagandizing?

March, 1969

MARRIAGE CONDITIONING

Mazal-tov!

This greeting is altogether in order in this season of weddings. Yet we know it in our bones that it is scarcely more than a greeting. It takes much more than wishes for good luck to make a marriage successful.

There is no hiding from the sins of our society and culture against marriage, but neither can we afford to overlook the failure of mothers and fathers to condition their childen for a happy matrimonial life. And "conditioning" is the verb, not "counselling." Counselling is something you do in a series of sessions. Counselling is something you do intellectually. Counselling is a kind of cram course which more often than not is useless. Conditioning is the verb. Conditioning is something you do over all the years when they are growing up. Conditioning is what you convey experientially. Conditioning is the whole character of your home life.

Along these lines, there are many things that parents ought to do *qua* parents. Let me, however, at the moment, focus merely upon one responsibility. To do their share in securing a successful marriage for their children, parents ought to take the pains to condition their young people in religion and in spiritual values.

A recent study has shown two and a quarter times less divorce amongst couples who practice religious worship. Kinsey's tables indicate twice as much infidelity in marriages without religious faith than in unions with it. Statistics of this ilk are only to be expected, because in our society the one great instrument for the cultivation of character and of the finest human values is religion, and religion alone. The very stuff of religion is the stuff of which successul marriage is woven.

It is somewhat amusing. Even the secularistic professionals in this field, who are almost exclusively sociologically and psychologically oriented, are given to talking in terms of the "sanctity" of marriage. Pray tell, what sanctity is there in life without a spiritual *weltanschauung*? Without faith, there cannot be that conception of the sacredness of the human being which makes real human love possible. It's not an accident that the majority of secularists in our midst still prefer to celebrate a marriage through the offices of a religious ministrant. It's a kind of acknowledgement that matrimony is not just a civil contract between two people. It's a hallowed compact between a man and a woman—"Kiddushin" as our tradition calls it, sanctification. People, however, need more than just a rite of blessings at the time of wedding. They need constant religious conditioning, something that will ever and always seize them with an awareness of their responsibilities and duties to the sacred spheres of life.

Everyone can use *mazal*. Everyone can use it, that is, if he is equipped with the tools to use it. There are no guarantees that we parents shall have *nachas*. But we can try it. We can condition our young people in the kind of life that will provide them with a capacity for *mazal*.

Mazal-tov!

June, 1969

THE ILLUSION OF INDEPENDENCE

Independent! What a glorious feeling!

Our craving for self-sufficiency is altogether understandable and even commendable; but it is not without its limitations. The striving for independence can be a misleading and detrimental goal. For at least three reasons.

In the first instance, independence is an impossibility, an illusion; and to strive after it is immature, is to get caught in the gossamer of make-believe. Remarks the Jewish Sage Ben Zoma: "Blessed be He Who created all these people to attend my needs. How much Adam had to toil! He had to plow and plant, cut and bind sheaths, thresh and winnow grain, grind and sift flours, and knead and bake, before he could eat a piece of bread. But I rise in the morning and find everything ready for me." Can one really live in a civilized and ordered society the way we do, every moment of the day benefiting from the toil and skill and knowledge of a whole galaxy of other human beings, and still feign something that borders on the air of self-sufficiency? What folly to speak of independence in the face of mankind's blatant interdependence.

Secondly, in addition to being self-deluding, the hankering for independence can well be self-impoverishing. Indispensable to the experience of love is the humility to be indebted to someone else for his or her expressions of affection. Yet there are people who, because of some misguided sense of independence, simply cannot be on the receiving end and accept endearments and niceties from others. It is not enough to love; one must be lovable. And this is what people who are propelled by a spirit of self-sufficiency cannot be. They deprive themselves of one of the greatest of life's gifts, human affection.

One sees an exemplification of this impoverishment, again, in the instance of people who pointedly refuse to associate with com-

169

pany that would broaden and elevate their persons, because such association would necessarily make them feel inferior and hurt their vanity. Too often we would rather be big fish in little ponds. The great Maimonides used to pray that he be cognizant of the superior knowledge of his colleagues, for, as he said it, "It is not given to me alone to see all that others see." I wonder how many people reading these words today would have been, in one phase or another of their lives, the wiser and richer if only they had not been so independent.

Finally, the pursuit of independence can prove costly, not only to the individual, but to the society in which he lives. Willy-nilly, we help shape the nature of our milieu. If, then, through some aberrant and misguided feelings of superiority on our part, we are impoverished people, inevitably we shall have so much the less to contribute to our community. Moreover, a society progresses and advances in proportion to the demands laid upon it by its members. We need people who aren't ashamed to be indebted to society, people who aren't too proud, too high and mighty, to expect things from their community. The self-sufficient citizen who needs nothing from his community contributes nothing to it.

This is the season of graduation, and many are the young men and women who will be going forth to carve out a place for themselves in this world. We wish them every success and achievement, and take the liberty, too, of counselling them not to try to be overly independent.

June, 1969

COLUMBUS DESERVES BETTER

"Hello, Rabbi Cohen?"

"Yes. Who's this?"

"You don't know me. I'm visiting in Montreal. My name is irrelevant. But, no doubt, you've seen me. I'm one of the characters in the wedding scene in 'Goodbye, Columbus.' I came upon your name in the phone book, so here I am calling you up. I hope you don't mind, Rabbi."

"Stop the kidding. Who are you, and what do you want?"

"Really, Rabbi. I'm one of those guests in the wedding scene in 'Goodbye, Columbus.' I want to get something off my chest. That's why I'm using this time between scenes to call you."

"What can I do for you?"

"Look who's calling the kettle black!"

"Me? I don't understand. I haven't said anything about that scene of yours in the picture."

"No, not you."

"You mean your creator?"

"Well, him, too. Look who can't stand our manners and is satirizing our behavior—the author of 'Portnoy's Complaint'! Poor Philip Roth; our coarseness is too much for such a refined individual. But, at the moment, I don't mean him so much as I do the others."

"What others?"

"You know, all those people who see the picture and come away from it justifying the satire. All those sensitive viewers who are embarrassed by the way we let ourselves go and carry on at the wedding party."

"Wait a moment there. You know, you can't blame them too much for their disgust. From where we sit, you don't exactly present the most edifying of sights."

171

"Granted, a bit on the crude side. But, Rabbi, how come all the comment is about that scene? How come, for example, there's so little vocalized disapproval of the behavior in the bedroom scene? Do you mean the way those young people carried on was more kosher than our gluttonous binge?"

"Well. . . ."

"But something else, Rabbi, and more to the point at the moment. You said, from where you sit. You should sit here with us behind the screen and behold the audience. Now that's an edifying sight! Fine and decent people, as it were, avidly watching dirty movies. Embarrassed by table piggishness, but so unruffled and nonchalant in a display of bed acrobatics. My my, how urbane and sophisticated we've become. *Tzu fressen* is scandalous, but to be a voyeur is respectable! Look who's calling the kettle black!

"You know something, Rabbi?"

"What?"

"Goodbye, Columbus?"

"Yes."

"No, Rabbi, A *klog tzu* Columbus!"

October, 1969

MORE THAN YOU CAN CHEW

Your intentions are good, and ambition teases you, too. Discretion, however, which is the better part of sagacity, dictates that you reckon with your limitations and square with reality. Why start something you can't finish? Why undertake something that is beyond you?

Well, discretion to the winds. It may be folly, but we are in a carefree mood and are urged to counsel—by all means, bite off more than you can chew. When an old reformer had his projects rejected on the grounds that they were impossible, he retorted, "Impossible? If that is all there is against them, let us go ahead." Beyond you? Perhaps, but the least you can do is to start and reach for it. And for a number of reasons.

A professional Swiss mountain guide once said to a group he was conducting: "I want you always to remember this—a mountain is never so high as from the bottom." That's true of all the mountains and obstacles and difficulties and challenges of life. They are most formidable and forbidding before we begin to tackle them. But once we begin to tackle them, once we commence the assault, for all the undeniable hardship they present, somehow they cease to be as insurmountable as before we began. Good intentions, but beyond you? Start, and it may not prove to be as defiant as you think.

More often than not, we don't know ourselves. We frequently air that fact in its negative sense. And, of course, it's true—we see everybody else's failings, we know what's wrong with everyone else; but we don't recognize our own faults. We don't know ourselves. There is, however, another side to this coin. If many don't know their own foibles, there are many who are not aware of their own virtues and strengths.

The average person is more capable than he readily believes himself to be. In every individual there resides a latent and untapped potential coated by rust for lack of engagement. We don't operate normally at our full capacity. Perhaps if we aspired and reached for that unattainable goal, we might manifest more ability than we ever contemplated having. Perhaps if we took the bite, we'd find that it's not more than we can chew.

There is something else involved here. When one begins something, he becomes willy-nilly involved and committed. Undertake, and, in a sense, you have put yourself under compulsion. And compulsion can elicit more dormant talent, can wring out more hidden power from an individual than anything else. Everyone has experienced this truth in his own being time and time again. Somehow, when we had no choice, when we got involved and it became our responsibility, when it was expected and demanded of us, somehow we did what we were convinced we could not do. Begin, get involved, and chances are that your commitment to the goal will inform your person with a new vitalizing resource and enable you to make the mark.

Resh Lakish, the Talmud records, used to say that if one starts out to do a worthy thing, the situation conspires to assist him.

There are so many things you'd like to do. But you're not going to kid yourself. You're afraid to bite off more than you can chew. Don't be so down-to-earth. After all, we have found out that, when man reached for the moon, he made it.

December, 1969

PILL TALK

It all happened quite accidentally. I'm not in the habit of eavesdropping. But standing there in the pharmacy, waiting for my Malox and saccharine tablets, I overheard a strange conversation. Emanating from one of the shelves and barely audible, it was a dialogue between two pills.

"Hi, Cyclamate. What are you doing here? I thought they got rid of you some time ago."

"Oh, hello there, Estrogen. They did make a clean sweep of my clan; but, in all this stock, they apparently didn't notice my jar, and so here I am. And I don't mind telling you, I'm plenty bitter."

"You, Cyc, a sweet thing like you, bitter?!"

"Cut the sarcasm, Estro. You know there is every reason in the world for me to have become a bitter pill. It's a hard thing to swallow—this pillocide that was so impetuously perpetrated against my compound. There wasn't even time for an appeal. All my friends and clients were caught short. Before they could mount a protest demonstration, the final solution was executed."

"I will admit that they rushed things a bit with you. But you didn't play it smart. From the very start, you should have gotten the Pope to ban you, the way he did me."

"What good would that have done?"

"You'd be surprised. In these anti-clerical and anti-religious times, any disapproval from that quarter would have generated a lot of counter-support for you and would have won you no little sympathy and popularity. But tell me, Cyc, how do you account for the fact that you were judged, condemned, and executed with such alacrity and without creating too much of a stir?"

"I'm not sure that I know how to explain it, Estro. But, for one thing, I figure that I'm the fall guy."

"The fall guy?"

175

"Exactly. I'm the *kaporah-hindel,* the scapegoat, for the guilt-feeling that is growing over the superfluity of pills in our day. In the wide galaxy of chemo-tablets, I'm the most innocuous. They can afford to get along without me. And so they have taken their piety out on my hide."

"Perhaps. But, Cyc, you have to confess that the scientists did find you unsafe."

"The scientists? That's one of the things that crumbles me most in this matter—my disenchantment with the scientists. I used to have so much faith in them. I was convinced that nothing, but nothing, could swerve them from the objective truth. But, forgive my boldness, Miss Estro, see how they have acted in your own instance. The U.S. Food and Drug Administration has officially rated you safe, in spite of overwhelming evidence that, healthwise, at least, you are anything but safe. How come?

"Isn't it because—no less than the author who has become a pornographer, and the actor who has turned exhibitionist, and the psychologist who sings the virtues of the new morality, and the rabbi who *hechsherizes* premarital relations, and the religious professor who theologizes in the pages of a lascivious magazine on reinterpreting traditional chastity in terms of the new promiscuity—no less than all the others, the scientist too has been swamped and swayed by the sexuality of our times. In our sex-obsessed age, the scientists haven't the guts to impugn you birth control pills. Don't tell me that something other than objective scientific judgment has not gone into your rating. What a joke—I'm *traif,* but you're kosher!"

January, 1970

A NEW BIGOTRY

Ageism.

If such a word doesn't exist, I am herewith coining it. We need a term for the new bigotry which has emerged on the contemporary scene.

At a time when, happily, racism has come under severe attack and is on the withering side, ironically a new venomous prejudice has erupted in our society and bids well to replace it in the dynamics of human hostility. While it's no longer kosher to dislike a person merely because of his color, it is altogether respectable, in certain circles, and even *de rigueur*, to contemn him merely because of his years. Older people, *a priori*, are regarded as inferior and reprehensible. Racism is out, but ageism is in.

Is it really a new bigotry? To be sure, conflict between the generations is hardly a novel phenomenon. Greek mythology bespeaks the antiquity of the antagonism. Even before there was man, as it were, the gods on their heights were having generational struggles. Uranus, the first ruler of the universe and father of the Titans, was wounded and dethroned by his youngest son Cronus. It wasn't long before the latter's son, Zeus, led his contemporaries against Pappa Cronus. In a terrible battle that lasted for ten years —the Titanomachy between the elder Titans led by Cronus on Mount Othrys and the younger Olympians led by Zeus on Mount Olympus—the father was overthrown and banished to a sphere of no consequence; and Zeus became the ruler of heaven and earth.

The young have always been jealous of the suzerainty of their adults and have always wanted to usurp their power. And I'm not so sure that this proclivity is such a bad thing. For, in the long run, it is this stripe of aspiration which makes continuity possible in the story of mankind and facilitates progress. It would, indeed, be a very sorry state of affairs if youth were devoid of the desire to take over and had no ambition to run things.

177

This kind of necessary generational conflict, however, is not what I allude to when I speak of ageism. The latter is, rather, nothing more than a frightening phenomenon of outright bigotry. It is a bias against the mature generation. It is a kind of perverted ideology—on principle, to begin with, you distrust and hate adults. If it's of the Establishment, you simply "know" that it's corrupt and no good. If it's of the older generation, you don't have to listen and find out, you are sure aforehand that it's worthless, passé, and insidious. Erikson complains that, while psychoanalysts at one time had to convince young people that they also hated their parents, today, they have difficulty in proving to them that they also really like them, in a way.

I allowed it was ironical to see the development of a new bigotry precisely at a time when an old one is on the way out, paradoxical to discern people closing their minds just when they seemed to have opened them. On the other hand, perchance it's not so enigmatic at that. Maybe there is a correlation between the two. Is it because people can't do without prejudice and bigotry that they adopt ageism when they eliminate racism?

And it's a profitable surrogate. Racism gives you only twenty million blacks on this continent to hate. Indulge in ageism—and think of all the millions you can hate!

February, 1970

HAVE YOU REALLY FAILED?

Defeat is not failure, and failure is not defeat.

In our fuzzy thinking, we often tend to obscure the difference between the two and treat them as one and the same phenomenon. For the sake of eschewing unwarranted feelings of guilt on the one hand, and for the sake of precluding irresponsible escapism on the other hand, it is important to draw a clear line of differentiation. Realism and integrity would dictate that we be more circumspect in our explications and evaluations.

Failure is a moralistic judgment and connotes criticism and aspersion. It suggests an inadequacy of response, a weakness that stems from within one's own person. Its premise is that one has not lived up to his potential, that he could have done more, that he could have behaved differently and better. Failure is a matter of culpability. It unavoidably implies that one is at fault and to blame.

Defeat is of a different order. It is an acquiescence to the reality that sometimes, for all my doing my best, the odds against me are too great. It's an acknowledgment of our basic limitations, of our impotence in the face of the impossible. Defeat has nothing to do with guilt. It's simply the sad fact that in life we are sometimes undone by overwhelming forces.

And often we smudge the line of demarcation between the two.

We do it commonly when we glibly hang the thing on the peg of tensions and pressures and the thrust of the times. This is not to deny that tensions and pressures and mores do exist. But then again, something else also exists. There is the stuff of our inner resources, character and will. When the deed is clever but less than honest and humane, is it a result of defeat—after all, that's the way the business world operates; or is it the consequence of failure? When mothers equip their single daughters with birth-control pills, is it because they are powerless before the new morality, or is it

179

because of some feeble fare in their parental role? Is the meagreness of our Jewish observances and commitment indicative of our defeat or our failure? One should assay the issues carefully and honestly and draw a line under the exact word.

"Where have I failed?" This is a tragic self-recrimination that rabbis often hear from the mouths of distraught mothers and fathers. Children don't always turn out the way we want them to, and, increasingly today, can be a source of unmitigated shame and pain. One is tempted to do the simplistic thing; to reason that, had the rearing been more scrupulous and effective, then the trouble could have been avoided. Perhaps. Frequently the blame lies with the sires and the adult generation. This is not, however, ever and always the case. For all the influence of the home, there are times when the forces of the hearth are no match for the sway and immoral tenor of society at large. Realistically, the home can be vanquished by the milieu and the environment. More often than not today, parents don't fail; they are defeated.

One of the favorite butts of contemporary criticism is the religious establishment. If religion is on a deep decline, surely it is because the synagogue has failed to keep up with the times. So runs the argument, when reduced to its essentials. If education today is in crisis and turmoil, it's because teachers and school have failed in their function. Perhaps. There is no gainsaying instances of that kind of failure. But we are dealing with more than just instances. We are dealing with a general state of affairs. And I genuinely wonder whether, in the overall picture, it is because the religious and educational establishments have failed or because they have been defeated.

Is it failure or defeat? One must distinguish between the two in order to know what to do about it.

January, 1971

KIDS AREN'T STAND-INS

Dear Rabbi Cohen,

I'm a teenager. Something has been bugging me of late, and I wonder if you would help me get it off my chest. I have a request to make of the grownups. Perhaps you can pass it on to them by way of your Bulletin column. Will you please tell the adults to stop making us kids their stand-ins.

Stop making us your religious stand-ins. Everyone everywhere today is harping about the "alienation" of youth from the synagogue. That's a big word—"alienation"—and I take it to mean that the kids aren't very interested in going to *shul*. And it's true. Most of my friends would consider a youngster a weirdo if he took *shul* seriously. On the few Sabbaths that I've attended, however, I've noticed that the adults aren't exactly crowding the synagogue either. I'm not particularly *shul*-minded myself, but neither are my parents, nor are their friends. After all, when I go skiing on Saturday mornings, I go with my folks. Why all this clamor about youth's alienation from the synagogue? Do you expect us to fill the *shuls* in your stead?

Both my parents are rather active on the Jewish community scene. I gather fom their laments that it's getting harder and harder to muster people for Jewish organizational work and causes. To hear them tell it, the majority of individuals today are indifferent to Jewish life and interested only in themselves and in their own pleasures. Why, then, the hangup on the kids' estrangement from Jewish life? Is it our job to carry the ball for Jewish solidarity?

My parents frequently get worked up over the kind of "language" I use. Granted, it isn't always the nicest. But did you read the other week, in *The New York Times* Sunday Magazine, about a psychiatric conference where one of the addresses given by a

181

famous psychiatrist was full of four-letter words? If it's O.K. in your sophisticated and arty circles, not to mention in current literature, why this disgust over "the language of modern youth"? Are we supposed to keep speech clean, while cultured grownups delight in obscenities?

And what about all this hypocrisy in the movie rating system? Here again, it appears that decency rests upon the shoulders of the under-eighteen, while "mature" folk can respectfully enjoy dirty movies. I sometimes think we should switch it around. Instead of the rule being "No children allowed unless accompanied by an adult," it should be "No adults allowed unless accompanied by a child." Perhaps in that way our entertainment world today would be very different, and pornography would not be part of the contemporary life-style.

You know, we aren't exactly blind to what goes on in that world of yours and to the adult "games" that you play. Is it logical, or even fair, to decry the morals of us young people when adults are so loose in their own? Don't expect us to be your fall-guys, tagged with the duty of guarding society's virtue, while you adults are AWOL from morality, getting your kicks and living it up.

I accept the charge that youth ought to be Jewishly committed —provided, that is, that we aren't your substitutes in that task. I agree that youth ought to be decent—provided, that is, you don't give us the job of being Mr. Clean and expect us to do your clean work for you. We don't like being stand-ins.

Sincerely,
A. D. Olescent

January, 1971

OF FISHES AND PONDS

The Graduate.

This is his season. From high school, from college, from professional school. I am well aware that the contemporary graduate is not altogether amenable to counsel from adults. *Au contraire,* he would tell us a thing or two. I, on my part, am ready to listen to him. But I would hope that, for all his own wisdom, he in turn is still open-minded enough to consider, at least, the distillation of accumulated experience. So I take my chances now and direct myself to the graduate.

Back in ancient Rome and Palestine, a proverb was current which advised: "Better be a head of foxes, than a tail among lions." We change the characters in the metaphor but aver much the same when we aphorize: "It's better to be a big fish in a little pond, than a little fish in a big pond." You want to be somebody? Then, don't overreach yourself; choose a more modest setting.

That sounds like good, down-to-earth, practical sense. Somehow, however, it doesn't capture the fancy of Jewish tradition. When, for example, Rabbi Mathithiah heard his fellow citizens mouthing the maxim, he turned the apothegm on its head and went around counselling: "Rather be a tail to lions, than a head to foxes." The Rabbi was of the persuasion that it's preferable to be a little fish in a big pond, than a big fish in a little pond.

And I think he's right. For a number of reasons. To begin with, to seek to be a big fish in a little pond is to be too patently and crudely rooted in sheer vanity. There is something dreadfully crass and obnoxious about a mentality which selects the stage of commitment wholly on the basis of the self-image it can project. If I may again change the characters in the metaphor, there is something repulsive about an individual who has to be top dog.

Secondly, please note—big splashes in little ponds, when all is

183

said and done, ring hollow. Samuel Johnson once said that, "Superiority of some men is merely local. They are great because their associates are little." There is something false and phony, something vacuous, about our own position when, to be a somebody, we have to surround ourselves with nobodies.

Thirdly, and most of all, it's not wise to prefer to be a big fish in a little pond, because a tack of that stripe dulls our potential and precludes us from developing our own maximum abilities. The potentialities latent in all of us need the goad of challenge and the impetus of competition and drive. When Robert Browning allowed that "A man's reach should exceed his grasp," he wasn't suggesting that we reach for the impossible, but only that we eschew the secure but unchallenging little pond and expose ourselves to the demanding but enriching currents of the big pond. The fact is that we are unfair to ourselves when, because of reasons of vanity or indolence, we limit our scope and insist upon being the head of foxes instead of a tail to the lions.

This, then, is my orientation. In what lies ahead—at the university, in the professional world, in every vocation—don't opt for the easier course. Don't settle for the less taxing pursuit, just because there you are sure to shine. Don't draw your circle of associates solely from among those in whose company you are comfortable without trying, and in whose midst you are by comparison great.

To the Graduate go my liveliest felicitations and sincerest wishes for every achievement.

June, 1971

LOVE FOR NOTHING

In our vocabulary, "prejudice" is a pejorative term. It connotes an unfair and ugly phenomenon. It suggests an adverse opinion that we form without just grounds, before we have sufficient knowledge. It belongs to the family of bigotry and hate.

That "prejudice" should have such a negative connotation for us is no little revealing. In reality, the word itself doesn't necessarily imply a hostile sentiment. All it actually means is a prejudgment, a conclusion drawn without adequate information. But might not that preconception be of a positive and friendly stripe? Might we not, without justification and sufficient verification, form a favorable opinion? Technically, one can be prejudiced for as well as against. "Prejudice," however, is rarely used in this kinder sense. For all intents and purposes, it is almost synonymous with "hatred," an unfounded and baseless antipathy. And it has come to have this lopsided meaning precisely because people generally hate for nothing, but rarely do they love for nothing. In forming an opinion, we are more prone to be hostile than to be friendly. We are more inclined—and that's all the word "biased" really means, to be inclined; and, yet, note that it has the same sinister ring as "prejudiced" does—to be against rather than in favor of. We are readier to hate for nothing than to love for nothing.

Why are we more apt to be prejudiced against than prejudiced for? I'm not sure that anyone has fathomed the answer to that bit of human perverseness. Moreover, I'm sure that the explanation, whatever it is, is quite complex. But some understanding of the phenomenon is surely available to us, if we but think on the matter for a moment.

To begin with, new encounters evoke the substratum of suspicion inherent in all of us. We are aware of the things to which we might sink, the indiscretions we might ourselves perpetrate;

185

and now, in evaluating the new encounter, we project these feelings. Because we are basically suspicious of ourselves and our own motivation, we are suspicious of the unknown and untried other.

Our greedy nature, too, plays a role in this story. We begrudge unearned approbation. It's the *quid pro quo* mentality wherewith we operate. If we are going to be generous with our sentiments, we want our magnanimity spent on the worthwhile. We are niggardly with our affections and are reluctant to waste them on the undeserving. Thus we find it safer to dislike than to like indiscriminately.

Our vanity is another factor. We are afraid of being duped and outsmarted; we have a fear of being made the fool, of being bested. At the bottom of it all lies our thraldom to prestige. We don't like to get caught backing the wrong horse, as it were; our pride would suffer in the instance of misplaced sympathy. Our vanity rebels at the prospect of being deceived; and so it's easier, when the ground is uncertain, to distrust than to trust.

Finally, there is in this whole concoction the element of our insecurity and inferiority. Have you ever noticed how you feel superior when there is someone or something that you can dislike and disdain? Hate, for all its ugliness, is a fascinating phenomenon. How we can strut, what big men we wax in our own eyes, when there are about us people and things we can dislike. Psychological study confirms that the most hating people in any society are those individuals who are bothered by feelings of insecurity and are exercised by a sense of inferiority. Sometimes it's bolstering to be prejudiced.

Observed the late saintly Rabbi Kook: If I hate people, it is altogether possible that I am mistaken; for a person is, after all, limited in his knowledge and liable to error. Hence the result might be that I would be guilty of hating somebody for nothing, guilty of unwarranted hostility. On the other hand, if, instead of hating them, I liked them and proved genial and friendly to them, what can be the worst that can happen? That they really didn't deserve my affection, and that I made the mistake of loving them for nothing? So what! It's better to love for nothing than to hate for nothing.

This strikes us as a rather good guideline for the year ahead.

We can be revolutionaries and turn the term on its head. We can metamorphose prejudice into trust. And in so doing, we can make 1970 a happier year.

December, 1969

ON MINDING ONE'S OWN BUSINESS

Nobody likes a busybody. The right to privacy is almost instinctual. This prerogative is all the more keenly felt in a democracy where individual liberty is of the very warp and woof of our existence. Indubitably, one of the basic guarantees of a democratic system is that we are all entitled to our privacy. It is quite natural, then, that in such an ambience a busybody is viewed with distinct disfavor. In the context of our social system, the right to privacy has as its correlative the duty to mind one's own business. Don't be a busybody, mind your own business.

Having said this, however, I hasten to note that the counsel is not as simple as it all sounds. To mind one's own business is not a clear-cut virtue, and the line between it and another trait of character, which is altogether uncommendable, is quite tenuous. The virtue of minding one's own business too frequently courts the danger of being a pietistic disguise for the vice of indifference. You do your duty, you fulfill your obligations, you take care of yourself; but beyond that, well, beyond that you mind your own business—which is another way of saying that it's not your concern and none of your business.

True, some things are not my business, and so I should mind my own. On the other hand, it is equally true that some things are so fundamental that they are my business. Because I am a human being, the way they treat blacks and Indians is my business. Surely we are not so calloused by our individualism that we don't feel the problem of nutrition in India. All hail the enlightened citizen who himself is free of all prejudice and bigotry; but is he quits with this, or is the anti-Semitism in his neighbors round about him his business, too?

Asked what he thought of the two candidates for the election, a perceptive voter replied, "Well, when I look at them, I'm thankful

188

only one of them can be elected." We are not revealing any secrets when we allow that the availability of qualitative leaders, whether it be in the area of government, or on the level of voluntary communal organizations, is becoming more and more limited. And understandably so. It's not that we are suddenly suffering from the dearth of capable individuals; there are plenty of talented people around. The fact is, however, we are not particularly a political-minded generation. And I use the last phrase in its best sense, in the sense of public-spirited. Our best talents are content to make the most of themselves in their respective fields; but beyond fulfilling their own personal obligations, they're not going to meddle, they're going to mind their own business. Is it really that—minding their own business? Or is it something more sinister and akin to indifference?

Perhaps in no area of our life are the morality and sagacity of minding our own business more pertinent than in the sphere of family living. There is no gainsaying this—for all our closeness to one another, each of us still has a right to his domain of privacy. There is room and room in every family for minding one's own business. But let's make sure it's only that and not just a cover-up for indifference.

So often we live together, yet in actuality are isolated from one another. A woman confided to me the other day that it was only after her husband took ill and she went into his business establishment that she appreciated, for the first time in her marriage, what her husband's day was really like. It's one thing not to interfere overly much in your child's life, but it's vastly different not to know what is going on and how that life is taking shape.

This is no appeal to become busybodies. But I am minded that sometimes, either innocently or not so innocently, we persuade ourselves that ours is the virtue of minding our own business, when, in reality, we are only indulging the vice of indifference and irresponsibility.

May, 1967

BUT NEITHER ARE WE SAINTS

"We are neither guilty of the peace of the wicked, nor are we to be credited with the sufferings of the pious." So allows Rabbi Jannai in the *Ethics of The Fathers*. He is saying that he and his ilk are neither reprobates nor saints. And that makes the Rabbi an abundantly honest individual.

For one thing, note that he is not falsely modest. He is not loath to highlight his virtue. He freely and even proudly acknowledges the fact that, unlike the wicked in his society, who are untroubled by the injustices of their world, he and his crowd are not at peace. Rabbi Jannai is honest. When credit is coming to him, he doesn't deny it; *au contraire*, he publicizes it.

Having been truthful in this respect, however, note it well, he goes on to be honest in another respect, too. He doesn't want to create the impression that, just because he and his coterie are not complacent reprobates, they are noble saints.

There's no denying the truth that the righteous necessarily suffer and anguish. Precisely because they are righteous they are afflicted with the *weltschmerz*. You really can't be a saint and not suffer. On the other hand, suffering per se doesn't make one a saint. And this is what Rabbi Jannai is so honestly pointing out—just because he and his company are troubled, that does not yet make them saints. They have no delusions about themselves. They are not evil like some, but that doesn't give them call to feel self-righteous. They can see, because they are free from the blinders of complacency, the inadequacies and sins and aberrations of the previous generation. Yet, they are honest enough to understand that, come another generation, and that younger generation will be able to point to plenty of faults in its sires.

Rabbi Jannai is honest. He admits that he does the right thing. But he is honest enough, too, to refrain from posturing as a saint.

190

All of which should point a lesson to a particular group of young people in our day. They begin honestly. They parade the truth that they can't, like others round about them, be at ease in the face of all that is wrong and corrupt in our society—poverty, war, racism, inequality. They are disturbed young people, and for this they irrefragably must elicit our commendation.

They are a far cry from those who created the *shtimmung* of the previous decade. Professor Donald Fleming described the 1950's as an era of "smothering complacency." It was also a decade par excellence when people unabashedly were hell bent in the pursuit of peace of mind. It was the era that saw the near apotheosis of the psychiatrist who was, after all, the great dispenser of peace of mind. Even on a higher level, it was an age that was smugly satisfied with itself and convinced that the best of all possible worlds was around the corner because of the brilliance of its scientific and technological achievements.

But all that has changed now. Suddenly, in a spurt of honesty, some in our younger generation have shaken us from our comfortable encapsulations. They have made us aware that our gross materialism has obfuscated so many of our human values, and that, more often than not, the road to hell is paved with good inventions. Suddenly, in a burst of probity, they are proclaiming that to be at ease at a time when beneath the glamorous veneer there is so much that is rotten is nothing short of the indulgence of the wicked. We have a troubled younger generation. And they're honest about it. They are not falsely modest; they know their involvement is their virtue. Hats off to them.

Here, however, is where a good many of them wax less than commendable and depart from the honesty of a Rabbi Jannai. They have taken to wearing a halo. Indeed, so blatant and strident has become their self-righteousness, that one becomes uncomfortably suspicious about their sincerity. One gets the impression of people who are eager to be troubled so that they can posture as saints.

It's one thing to be righteous, but God forfend us from the self-righteous. There is none so limited in his vision as the self-righteous. There is none so callous, inconsiderate and cruel as the self-righteous. There is none so intolerant and authoritarian, and, indeed, totalitarian and tyrannical as the self-righteous. And that is what is so frightening about the contemporary scene. Ours is the spectre of righteous young people transmuting into Frankensteins of self-righteous saints.

It is wonderful to surmount the complacency of the wicked and be righteously involved, points out Rabbi Jannai; provided that, in so doing, you don't delude yourself into thinking that you are a saint.

August, 1969

TOO FAR EAST IS WEST

There is a tendency in many people to make a special effort in order to compensate for their deficiencies, a propensity to make up for their weaknesses. Now this is all very fine and even commendable, but the rub is that sometimes they are inclined to overdo it. They overcompensate. And as with all instances of excess, we can do more harm than good with overcompensation.

I heard it said recently of a man who had suddenly seen the light that, for the first time, he saw his duty and overdid it. All cheers for repentance, and hail to the man who has the guts to acknowledge his foibles and set out to compensate for his mistakes. And I agree, too, with Ralph Waldso Emerson that "Nothing great was ever achieved without enthusiasm." Only, we are reminded now that there is wisdom in appreciating that too much zeal can spell out folly rather than valor. "My zeal has undone me," cries King David in one of the Psalms. I like the way Arthur Guiterman phrases it: "Remember always, too far East is West." That's the way it goes with overcompensation—too far East is West.

I don't know if anyone would be happy to live in a milieu of Victorian prudery and hypocrisy. Looking back now, we can understand how wanting in healthy truthfulness and realism that era was. Yet, looking at our own times, we begin to feel that the modern spirit is not only compensating but overcompensating. Ours has been aptly described as a sex-saturated society. By all means, let us espouse an approach of candor. I suggest, however, that when truthfulness is equated with obscenity and realism with licentiousness, when the doffing of hypocrisy becomes nothing less than the sanction of immorality, then the modern spirit is not compensating for a prior failing, but overcompensating, and is therewith undermining the whole fabric of our family and social life.

Too far East is West. As is very often the case today with our

193

attitude towards children. There indubitably is a tyranny in the policy where children are to be seen and not heard. There is no soundness in ignoring the individualism of a child. Haven't we, however, gone overboard in the other direction, when, in the rearing of our children, we wallow in excessive indulgence and unrestricted permissiveness? It's one thing to allow children to be heard; it's quite another thing to regard them as policy makers and the equals of adults. The evils of our overcompensation in this instance are evidenced all around us and are well documented in The Hechingers' study entitled *Teenage Tyranny*. Apparently some among us saw their duty and overdid it.

Don't push too far in order to make up for a failing. King Solomon recognized the self-defeating character of overcompensation when he counselled: "Be not righteous overmuch; neither make thyself overwise; why shouldst thou destroy thyself." Perhaps the temptation is greatest when it comes to correcting our personal traits.

Is it a streak of cynicism in you that you are overcoming? Of course, there is some good in the worst of people; but aren't you going a bit too far when, in reaction now, you can see no faults in anybody. Disingenuousness is no substitute for cynicism and the supression of our critical apparatus boots no one any good. By all means, get rid of your shyness, but don't make the mistake of replacing it with aggressiveness. Your niggardliness is well done away with, but don't succumb to prodigality. A man ought to stand on his own two feet, but arrogance is hardly an improvement over dependency. Whatever the gap in our character, let's not make the mistake of overcompensating.

October, 1974

THERE IS NO HIDING

There is the waggish observation that if Adam were to return to earth, the only thing he would recognize would be the old jokes. May I add, not only the old jokes, but also the old errors and mistakes. And perhaps, in a kind of sardonic way, they are one and the same, old errors and old jokes. I have the feeling that the oldest error, or the oldest joke, that Adam would recognize is the one entitled "He Should Have Known Better."

I say it's the oldest and one that Adam would surely recognize, because our common ancestor himself was its author; and, to boot, he sired it early in his career. "Where art thou?" comes the derisive voice of the Lord. Adam had disobeyed the will of God; and to eschew the consequences of his misdeed, he sought to conceal himself among the trees of the garden. What a joke! What a mistake! Adam thought he could hide. He had just eaten from the Tree of Knowledge, he had just become a reasoning and rational creature; and for all that, he thought he could hide from the truth, he thought he could escape from reality. He should have known better.

It's the oldest joke in the books and we're still repeating it. Down deep, we really know better. It's just that, face to face with an unpleasant prospect, we act as if we had never eaten from the Tree of Knowledge. We become irrational and try to hide from the truth. We are primarily afraid of the changes that a confrontation with reality will demand of us. Most of us prize the status quo. This is our great comfort, this is our private Garden of Eden—the kind of living we are used to, the way things are. Change necessarily is fraught with uncertainty, inevitably it entails readjustment. Why can't we leave well enough alone? Simply because truth and reality are no respecters of ease and comfort. To hide from this fact of life is to court folly.

195

And we try to hide in a variety of ways. We call into play all kinds of alibis. We invoke neutrality and pretend we're not involved. We delude ourselves and wallow in self-deception. We do more, in order to hide from the truth and keep from disturbing our status quo. We bury our heads in the sand and indulge in willful ignorance. "The worst sort of hypocrite and liar," wrote Hilaire Belloc, "is the man who lies to himself in order to feel at ease." What an egregious joke to think we can hide from reality.

We are living in revolutionary times; and whether we like it or not, and for all the inevitable altering of our wonted pattern of living, there is no hiding from the truth that we are living in an integrating world. We shall have to make room in our scheme of things for peoples and races who heretofore have not been part of our Garden of Eden. Someone once observed that a conservative is a person with sense enough to know that change isn't necessarily progress. I go along with that kind of sanity. But by the same token, it is absurd to try to thwart the essential dynamic quality of life. For all our commitment to traditionalism, there is no blinding ourselves to the truth that we must make room in the framework of our religion for development and change.

What stupidity to think we can hide from reality. Who was it that said that a person begins to lie about his age when his face begins to tell the truth about it? The best thing to do with our grey hairs is to learn to respect them. I suppose one of the most difficult ideas to get used to is that children not only grow up but grow away from us. The wisdom of letting go is a compelling necessity. We're all tempted to rationalize our faults of character and personality, but ultimately there's no covering them up. Far better to face ourselves squarely and honestly.

We hide not only from our failings but from our capacities as well. To know our abilities is so often to disturb our laziness and ease. Many are the persons who are willfully oblivious to their talents for leadership, simply because it is more comfortable and uninvolved that way. We should know better; we can't hide from our gifts without impoverishing and damaging our persons.

How much can you afford to give? There are people who don't want to know how much they can really afford; it might mean changing their whole pattern of giving. But conscience will not be thwarted. We ought to know better; there's no hiding from the truth.

Adam was a fool; he tried to hide. But elsewhere in the Bible, to the challenging question "Where art thou?" comes the resolute answer, "Here am I." That should be our answer, too.

October, 1964

DON'T SNUB THE COMMON

The masses.

Does that term ring in for you a note of condescension and even disdain? In this respect, one is reminded of Rabbi Akiba's observation that it was only for the sake of the people that God spoke to Moses their leader. There is in our Tradition a very palpable and basic respect for the common and ordinary. "Always respect the public," is the counsel of the Sages. The common is not as common as we sometimes tend to think.

Consider this matter with reference to the low esteem with which we are wont to hold the taste of the masses. Granted, when one examines the fare of public entertainment and popular culture, one cannot but conclude that tastewise the public does not shine. But there is a vicious fallacy involved here. The stuff of our mass media and world of entertainment is of low calibre, not because the public is incapable of appreciating something better, but only because those who furnish the diet have little or no regard for the capacities of the audience. It is they who dish out the pap which has become identified as popular taste. Everyone will concur that the Prophets provided us with poetry at its rarest. And yet these Prophets addressed their words not to the highbrows of their day, but to the common folk in the streets of Samaria and Jerusalem. It is almost difficult for us to appreciate today that Shakespeare wrote for the populace, and not for literature students at Oxford and Cambridge. If we had a high regard for ordinary people and their capacities, indubitably, the whole realm of popular taste would be of a higher level.

Think again how we manifest disrespect for the common by the prevalent vogue of deriding conformity and the conventional. Indeed, this last word has taken on a disparaging connotation. The sophisticated tenor of our society prefers the unconventional, and, in its schematics, the most odious offense is conformity.

To be sure, conformity becomes an evil when it obliterates worthwhile individualism. Our aim, however, at the moment is at those who would arrogate status by disingenuously rising above the conventional. It matters not that the morals and mores of the general society may in themselves be more commendable and conducive to a healthy and decent life; they're above the conventional, they're different, those morals and mores are not for them. Unconvenality today is too often a specious status symbol.

See, finally, how our contempt for the ordinary expresses itself in a posture of profundity. The art here lies in going beneath the surface. It's a kind of pseudo-analytic, pseudo-psychological explanation in which the apparent and obvious give way to something "deeper" and usually more sinister and cynical. David and Jonathan were more than just the superb friends that the Bible makes them out to be, runs the smart view; they were homosexual lovers. Your neighbor is not charitable because he's generous and idealistic, but really because of a deep-seated compulsive quirk or guilt complex. Students fail in their school work, not because they are lazy and indolent, but because they are acting out their hostility against their parents. There is no attempt here to deride depth motivation which, in many instances, offers the only true and sound explanation. We are, however, irritated by the ease and glibness with which some people distort the apparent and real just for the sake of playing brilliant and posturing profound.

I like Boerne's statement that "You should have education enough so that you won't have to look up to people; and then more education so that you will be wise enough not to look down on people."

May, 1974

LOSING MY COOL

Ouch!

The exclamation burst from me all right.

But it wasn't because the endodontist had struck a sensitive spot in my mouth. In fact, it wasn't even I who sat on his chair. It was another member of my family.

I was empathizing, feeling her ache in my jaw—an instance of his calibre in the first instance. Moreover, he wasn't out of line. ination was quite painless. And that's all it really was. He didn't work on the tooth, he just examined it—for the purpose of giving an estimate for "the job."

Aha, an estimate! That's what wrung the ouch from me? You're getting warmer. I don't mind telling you the price he mentioned was a whopper and stunned me. Then and there, I was passionately for denticare. He wasn't even an oral surgeon, but he wielded no mean expertise in the art of *reissen*. One had to have a lot of nerve, I smarted to myself, to charge such fees just for killing a nerve.

Yes, I very much felt like yelling out when the estimate was re-layed to me. And I would have, except that I was retrained by members of my family. I was stifled. I had no right to be so in-dignant and complain. No one compelled me to suggest a specialist of his calibre in the first instance. Moreover, he wasn't out of line. That, I was assured, is the going rate nowadays. It is the accept-able standard. And didn't I appreciate that this is a free society and a professional has the liberty to charge what he wants? No, I was menacingly warned, I should be the mature person I'm sup-posed to be and not sound off.

Well, that did it! It wasn't the estimate that extorted it from me. It's this "maturity," this sophisticated stoicism which would have me hurt and not cry out that makes me explode now. I'm burning, and I'm supposed to keep my cool. Ouch!

200

Gerald Sykes calls us "The Cool Generation." Underneath we're nothing of the sort; underneath we're anything but calm and collected. But it's *de rigueur*, we dare not "over-react." You don't "ouch," even *ven es tut vay.*

You don't ouch when, roundabout you, you see phoniness brazenly displacing genuineness. You don't ouch when, with much glee and vulgarity in their delineations, "Jewish" writers defame Jewish life. You don't ouch when, with public participation, the ambience of our society is polluted and gutterized. You don't ouch when, gallingly, villains are celebrated as heroes. You don't ouch —you keep your cool and take it in your stride.

The other day, in my study, a father unburdened himself of a very lugubrious story concerning his daughter. And when I asked him why he hadn't exerted more paternal willfulness, I got the usual answer. You don't register too much displeasure with the kids nowadays. You play it cool and ride it out with them. Parents can be bursting inside, but they dare not utter an ouch.

Recently, I was reprimanded by a young man who had heard me declare publicly that I would not officiate at an intermarriage. And, indeed, I must grievously report that a kind of "broadmindedness" is apparently beginning to overtake some of my colleagues themselves. It boots Judaism no good, they have it, for rabbis to "over-react" and get "hung-up" on intermarriage. Ouch!!

I don't know what good it does. I have a feeling it's not altogether futile—if only it relieves me. But when it hurts, I want to exercise my right of free expression in this free society. When it hurts, I insist upon "ouching."

October, 1972

PESSIMISM WITHOUT CYNICISM

In many respects, life is a losing game.

Beguile ourselves as we may, we cannot wishfully think away the inevitable defeats that lie at the core of our human existence. Isn't this raw pessimism? Indeed, it is. But it butters no parsnips to decry it. Pessimism is more than a mood, more than a subjective phenomenon. It springs from the very nature of things, warranted by reality, and has, therefore, objective validity.

Let's make this clear. Faith, religious faith, has no quarrel with pessimism. This will undoubtedly sound strange to many because of the trend to regard it the very function of religion to dispel unease, dispense happiness, and infuse a sense of power and confidence. Unfortunately, in many quarters, belief has been reduced to a kind of roseate delusion that all a person has to do is to get hold of himself and he will emerge happy and victorious. It is an immature conception woven of gossamer fancy. The purpose of religion is not to delude and disguise the unpleasant. Whatever else it seeks to do, it is the function of faith to recognize the justified pessimism of life, and then, acknowledging it, keep this pessimism from degenerating into cynicism. Oscar Wilde once defined a cynic as a man who knows the price of everything and the value of nothing. It is one thing to aver that life is a losing game—that's pessimism. But quite another thing, based on that premise, to conclude, therefore, that the game is not worth the struggle—that's cynicism. Ours is to engage in the contest, even in the face of certain defeat, "to love the game beyond the prize." Faith at its effective best is the stamina to be a pessimist without being a cynic.

The thanklessness of leadership is a disconcerting fact but, nevertheless, inveterate in human society. Do we, therefore, for all our ability eschew involvement, because in the end we are bound to be hurt? Or do we have the stamina "to love the game beyond the prize" and play even if we lose? To be kind, even if we're sure to get it in the neck? To be an idealist, knowing full well that every ideal goes awry when translated into concrete reality?

It is in the nature of growing up that children do not accord their parents the appreciation they have merited. The rearing of a family is replete with disappointments and frustrations. To cite those instances where people purposefully deny themselves offspring or keep their family small, because, as they explain, parenthood in the end is a thankless enterprise, may be an illustration *ad extremum*. But there is the concept of "emancipated parenthood," something which has much wider currency today, the feeling that one should not be overly devoted and self-sacrificing. "Don't be a fool," is the cant. "Don't give so much of yourself. In the end it doesn't pay."

Sacrificial devotion to the family is the duty of parenthood, regardless of its being in large measure a losing game. And if that phenomenon has become watered down, it is not because we have become "smarter" today, but because we have allowed ourselves to be demoralized into cynicism.

"Perforce thou wast born, perforce thou wilt die." Surely we cannot cavalierly dismiss the pessimism engendered by reflecting on man's finitude. Strive and struggle, and then, death. What a cruel and losing game! But here is the acid test. Does it demoralize us? Esau sold out his birthright because, as he said, behold I'm surely going to die. I wonder how many talents have gone awasting, how many people did not become the individuals they might have been, since the final pay-off did not justify for them the struggle. Our human birthright is to make the most of ourselves. Do we espouse the philosophy of "eat, drink, and be merry, for tomorrow we die," and thus sell it out? It's all the same in the end, so what difference does it make whether we play black or white, unfairly or fairly, indecently or decently, selfishly or altruistically? Here it is, pessimism turned into a cynicism that would obliterate all morals and values and standards. And I am reminded of Israel's Sages who, after a debate, concluded that though it were better for man not to have been created, let him heed his deeds. For all the strikes against him, let him play the game like a man.

This is faith at its best—the strength to take our pessimism without cynicism.

November, 1972

IN THE DISGUISE OF LOVE

Is it love? Or is it really selfishness?

"To create love," writes Dr. Karl Menninger, "we must begin by sacrifice." That goes to the heart of an ironic matter. Incongruous as it may seem, often what purports to be love is, in actuality, only so much unwitting selfishness. To achieve the genuine article, we must be ready to pay a costly price. Real love demands true selflessness.

There's an amusing story told about a man who, returning home after a difficult day at the office, found his two youngsters unbearably boisterous. He scolded them severely and sent them off to bed. The next morning he found a note pinned to his bedroom door. It read, "Be good to your children and they will be good to you. Signed —God."

Sometimes being good to dear ones is motivated not so much by our concern for them as it is by our concern for ourselves. We want to be liked by them, and, consequently, we fear doing anything that might disrupt our favorable standing with them. If you will, it's a kind of bribery to win their affection and maintain a preferred position in their sight. Granted, the "good fellow" who overlooks faults and indulges failings is apt to avoid painful moments when anger and dislike are incurred. But surely if we are sincerely more concerned for our loved ones than for ourselves, then we shall, for all the temporary affection it loses us, correct where correction is in order, criticize where criticism is called for, speak the truth where truth will better and improve. "For whom the Lord loveth He correcteth, even as a father the son in whom he delighteth."

The most obvious form of selfishness disguised as affection is instanced by possessive love. And we need not betake ourselves to aberrant extremes to discern the phenomenon. There's a tinge of it in the parent who resents his child's giving more attention to his circle of friends than to his family. There's a measure of it, too, in the mother who, for all her surface nicety, down deep harbors a prejudice against the young lady who "stole away" her son's heart. As a husband or wife, have you ever chafed at sharing your spouse's attention with some society or organization or cause? Have you ever complained about "playing second fiddle"? How narrow and impoverishing is the kind of affection that selfishly seeks to restrict and monopolize. The price of real love inevitably calls for the ability to share the attention and interest of dear ones with others.

Perhaps nowhere is selfishness more at play in family relationships than in the tendency to submerge the individuality of a loved one and mould him in one's own image. Here's a father who is sparing no effort to make his son a lawyer, here's a mother for whom nothing is too hard to afford her daughter the right setting. It's not that these young people are so keen about their parents' choice, nor do they necessarily have especial talents along those lines. But mother and father are convinced. These are the things they had always wanted. If they were to live again, that's exactly what they would choose for themselves. It doesn't require too much profundity to realize that in spite of all the good intentions and sacrifice, what we have here is not really love, but essentially an unquenchable passion to fulfill oneself and one's own dreams vicariously through the medium of children. It is basically nothing more than a selfish desire for personal gratification. Ambitiousness for dear ones is not always an indication of devotion. There is no genuine love where we cannot sacrifice our will in deference to the other's individuality.

Finally, consider this fact. If yours is going to be more than a selfish experience, you must not only harbor affection, you must, in turn, be the kind of person whom others can have the pleasure of loving. You don't really love, unless you can be loved. A young woman once asked her baby nurse what was the most difficult thing for a young mother to learn. She replied, "That other people have perfect children, too." I have a friend who was reared by a mother who had eyes only for her son. Today his attachement for her is not all that it might be, because, as he frankly explains, that kind of smallness embarrasses him. We can hold in endearment only those whom we can respect; and small people, even if they are our kin, down deep don't excite our esteem. Do we really think that, in our zeal to provide for dear ones, we can demean character and sacrifice ethics and principles and social responsibility, that we can forget about ourselves and the rest of the world, and still proffer them a meaningful relationship? This is the price of real love—you can't be so selfish as to neglect yourself and live only for your beloved.

This devotion of yours that you call love—is it the genuine thing, or only selfishness in disguise?

December, 1972

FIRST IMPRESSIONS

It's the kind of counsel that rings familiarly in our ears. In one guise or another, we're always hearing it, and often verbalizing it ourselves, too. "It's the first impression which people get of you that counts." The importance of making the right impression; and making it early in the game, because later it may be too late.

In more detached and morally rarified moments, one balks at this need to discharge impressions. There seems to be something degrading about it all. One would devoutly wish that human dignity could be spared the ravages of Carthaginian crassness and that we did not have to sell ourselves all the time. Would that we didn't have to be so preoccupied with making impressions.

But there's something else involved here. Aren't we being too cynical when we lay it all on the threshold of commercialization? In the last analysis, making impressions is inevitable, because there is no human perception that does not carry with it an element of judgment. Like it or not, we are always judging, always evaluating, always appraising. We don't just see, we see and at the same time register a value judgment. We don't just hear, we hear and at the same time approve or disapprove. It's the critical faculty at work in man, without which there would be no direction in our lives. Perhaps you call it discernment; but whatever its term, it is that compass in our perception of the world round about us which keeps us from drifting and enables us to relate to our environment with meaning and purpose. If impressions are inevitable, it is because man is essentially a judging creature.

Making the right impression is important; but so, too, is its reciprocal, reading the impression rightly. Stuart Chase says that prejudice can be defined as a judgment which does not change, and is impervious to facts and reason. He cites the example of an Oxford student who candidly remarked, "I despise all Americans but

I have never met one I didn't like." The pitfall of bias is always there, and, at the moment, even too commonplace to excite our attention. There is, however, another snare in this whole area of our judgments. Paul Tournier, the distinguished Swiss physician and psychiatrist, in his book *The Meaning of Persons,* incisively notes that sometimes the very judgments we pass keep us from really knowing the object of our judgment. This is not a matter of prejudice; it borders more on jumping to conclusions, on sufficing with early impressions. Our critical faculty boomerangs. Instead of enabling us to penetrate appearances, it deceives us and denies us access to the real core.

The losses we incur and the injustices we perpetrate through our snap judgments! Surely it is part of everyone's experience to regret, because of some impression or other, "not having got to really know him sooner." We do it all the time in our organizational life. Many are the individuals who are "discovered" unforgivably late in the game, because opinion has foolishly led us to underestimate them. I wonder how many readers of this column have never really gotten to know their synagogue because of impressions that they've had. Make a good impression, by all means. But be circumspect, too, in how you read your impressions. Don't let your judgments ever get in the way of your really knowing.

October, 1965

THE LINE OF MOST RESISTANCE

Given the choice between the easy and the difficult, we tend to select the easy thing to do. Where there is an alternative, we go for the cheaper way out, the quicker way. We prefer the slighter task, the lesser responsibility. We take the line of least resistance.

That's what makes Ben Azzai's counsel so puzzling. "Be swift," admonished the Sage in the *Ethics of the Fathers,* "to perform an easy precept." Why prompt us towards the facile? If there's any urging that's required, surely it is for the weightier things and not for the lighter ones. You don't have to encourage us to choose the easier course; quite instinctively we go for the line of least resistance.

But do we now? Sometimes our trouble is that we take, not the line of least resistance, but the line of most resistance. What is it —vanity and exhibitionism, absolutism, exaggerated perfectionism, a black and white mentality—that motivates people to insist upon the harder course, the costlier way, the heavier burden, the bigger responsibility? In and of itself, there is nothing wrong with this tack, and often it is even most commendable. To undertake the bigger challenge is praiseworthy, and to aspire to higher goals is admirable. But here's the rub: Frequently, people will concentrate so zealously and exclusively upon the larger attainment that, not only do they fail to attain it, but lose out as well on the smaller one. Obsessed with the major, they neglect the minor achievements that might have more readily been theirs. Out for all, they get nothing. Thus Ben Azzai counsels, "Be swift to perform an easy precept." Don't disdain the more modest opportunity in deluded anticipation of the greater one.

In the pursuit of happiness, don't surrender the smaller joys of life for the allure of the grander pleasures. I know a man who slaved and hoarded and stinted the better part of his days, in order to build himself a dream house. In the end, he enjoyed not even an average home that might all along have been his. She's a foolish woman, isn't she, who holds out for the luxury garment and ends up perforce with the simpler one from which she could have benefited long before. People will cheat themselves of the delights and enrichment of theatre and concert by insisting that, if they can't afford the best seats, they won't go at all. Do you rue that stubbornness which led you to wait for a real vacation and finally deprived you even of the smaller holidays that could have been yours?

Don't forego modest achievement for the dubious promise of some exciting accomplishment. How trenchant Longfellow's observation that "Most people would succeed in small things, if they were not troubled by great ambitions." In the creative field, I wonder how many books have not been written because their potential authors were bent upon being Faulkners or nothing. Many there are, I'm sure, who could have chalked up some measure of success in the business world, had they not held out so long for the great opportunity. There are any number of individuals within my own ken who might be of some service to our community, were it not for their desire to be of the most service.

Don't sacrifice the partial answers by demanding conclusive solutions. The reality of our times evinces scant hope for any basic settlements that would relieve the cold war. This fact, however, should not induce us to join the ranks of the political "fundamentalists" who would discourage negotiations on anything but the root of the impasse. If we can't have the major solutions, shall we not even benefit from minor agreements? I applaud idealists, but question the approach of those who are so obsessed with world betterment that they have no heart for the easier possibility of making their own more limited community a better place to live in. Education, in the last analysis, is the indispensable key to brotherhood. But pending that long and decisive process, are we to relinquish the readier, if only partial, alleviations offered by the instruments of law and statute? By all means, go out and save the world. But while doing that, don't let your big goal of the perfect salvation keep you from multiplying little and partial salvations. "Be swift," said Ben Azzai, "to perform an easy precept."

May, 1958

GIVE LUCK A CHANCE

"The fault, dear Brutus, is not in our stars,
But in ourselves, that we are underlings."

No, Brutus, don't ascribe it to the sway of the stars, don't attribute it to luck. For all that people have constant reference to it, there is no such thing as luck. It's an illusion; it has no substance or objective reality. Connoting opposite things to different people, it's such a relative term that it doesn't really mean much of anything. A young boy once asked his father what luck is. "Luck, my son," explained the experienced parent, "is something that enables another fellow to succeed where we have failed." Very often it's only that—a happy fiction to soothe our envy and wounded vanity, an excuse for our own inadequacy, a comforting belittlement of our neighbor's achievement. "We make our own fortunes," said Disraeli, "and we call them fate."

At least, that's what I would like to believe; that's what I would like to preach. What a vigorous and stirring idea, what a hopeful and encouraging promise! Man is master of his own fate, and there is no such thing as luck. But will it as I may, common experience thwarts me. Round about me there is too much evidence of fate. There are people who are just simply dogged by misfortune, while others are always getting the breaks. "If a man is destined to drown," says a Jewish proverb, "he will drown even in a spoonful of water." And conversely, states yet another proverb, "Throw a lucky man into the sea, and he will come up with a fish in his mouth." Think wishfully as we may, can we in all truth, with arrogance and cocksureness, allow that there are not areas beyond our control, circumstances beyond our reach, that manipulate our lives and shape our destinies? It may not be in the stars, there may be no goddess of Fate; but surely this fact is overwhelming—the breaks we get or don't get aren't always of our doing. We need a little bit of luck.

Bow to fate, or whatever it is you call by some other name. But don't stop there. For the irony of the matter is that luck itself needs some luck. It needs the right material to work with. In a discussion the other day, someone remarked that England was lucky to have survived the German blitz. Luck, undoubtedly, but something more, too. In England, luck had the chance of working with a Churchill who said and a British people who heard and responded to—"Let us so bear ourselves that if the British Commonwealth and Empire last for a thousand years, men will still say, 'This was their finest hour.'" There were many circumstances and factors beyond Jewish control which destined the creation of the State of Israel. But those circumstances had a break, too—they had a settlement of Jews in Palestine, they had a Haganah, they had a World Zionist Movement. That felicitous hour of history had something to work with. Luck is a wasted and sterile affair unless you give it a chance.

A woman in my study was unburdening herself of her problems. She was, above all else, racked by a terrible sense of loneliness. She spoke enviously of a certain neighbor who "was lucky because she had so many friends." I tried to explain to her that, in this respect, she had as much luck as her neighbor. The trouble was that she wasn't giving the opportunity for friendship an even break. Unlucky in marriage? There is no gainsaying that homes founder because of forces beyond the control of the parties. In many instances, however, the failure is not due to the absence of luck. Ofttimes all the ingredients of success are there, yet it doesn't work; a failure because fortune doesn't have the kind of people with whom it can cooperate. You don't always have luck. But this is what hurts, having it and not giving it a chance.

Did you ever hear someone say, or perchance voice it yourself: "Oh, he's lucky, he has religion to lean on"? If you were to live in certain other countries and say that, I could understand. But, when you are blessed to live in this free country and fortunate enough to have around you so many opportunities for becoming at home in religion, one can only conclude that it's not a matter of chance at all; it is, rather, a matter of not giving your chance the break to work with you. Wendell Phillips envied the faith of a devout Negro woman. "I would give you some to take home with you," she said, "if you had anything to put it in."

This is graduation season. We wish our young men and women who are setting out on their careers and vocations good luck. For, well equipped as they are, their future in goodly measure will depend on the stars. We wish them, then, luck. But more than that, we wish that they give their luck a chance.

June, 1958

DON'T DISLIKE THE SUPERIOR

Learn to live with it.

That kind of counsel is not easy to take. At first hearing, it sounds a dismaying note of finality and hopelessness, a dreadful realization that the difficulty cannot be removed and must remain. There doesn't seem to be too much solace or answer in that kind of a solution. Actually, however, learning to live with it connotes more than just the acceptance of the inevitable. Far from the advice of resignation, it's a call for that extra inner strength which would prevent our disabilities from distorting our whole persons and bemeaning our beings. It means a hard thing, but an essential one. It means limiting the damage of our afflictions.

Learn to live with jealousy. Save we be saints, envy is a disease that afflicts each and every one of us. And there is no gainsaying its deleterious nature. The Rabbis did not exaggerate when they said that it can destroy a man's whole world. It is rightfully decried by every religious tradition. Yet, in all truth, can we hope to eradicate jealousy from the human being? It is, is it not, an incurable innate weakness, a disability that we must bear as long as we live. We can't eliminate envy. But this we can and must do: We can learn to live with it.

For jealousy is one thing, unavoidable and ineluctable. What it does to us, however, is quite another thing, preventable and remediable. Above all else, it has a way of propelling us to dislike and to hate. When we are jealous of someone, we almost invariably, in addition, dislike or even hate that somebody. This correlation between envy and animosity is quite understandable. A person who provokes our jealousy implies a comparison that underscores our inadequacy. He shows us up, as it were. Compared to him, we are inferior. Moreover, he presents us with a challenge. If he can achieve such and such, why should we not be able to do as well? To

214

meet the challenge, however, would require on our part greater effort and striving, a change in our easy and comfortable pace. It would mean a lot of trouble and bother. "The envious praise only that which they can surpass," remarked Colton. "That which surpasses them they censure." The fact of the matter is, we abhor comparisons that delineate our weaknesses, we resent challenges that disturb our peace. Thus, quite understandably, we dislike and even hate that which causes our jealousy. This is the nub of the matter. To be sure, you can't rid yourself of enviousness, but you can keep it from distorting your character. Learn to live with your jealousy—in essence it means this, don't allow it to bedevil you into disliking the superior.

That sounds rather strange, disliking the superior. On the contrary, do we not admire it? In a way we do, but very often we do not. We admire greatness, yet, make no mistake about it, we hate it, too. Nothing delights many people more than the uncovering of some weakness in a great figure that will downgrade his stature. Not so great after all, not so superior to us. That's our secret comfort. Is it sheer sympathy that makes us automatically take sides with the underdog? Or is there something more selfish and twisted, our dislike for the upperdog, that is also a factor? There may be no reason in the world to contemn him—on the contrary, every reason to esteem him; but, all things being equal, we don't like the wealthy man. How pertinent the injunction to judges not only not to show favoritism to the wealthy, but also to harbor no prejudice against them. Men in public service constantly incur the gratuitous enmity of the populace. More than a little contempt for the educated person is frequently voiced with the phrase "highbrow."

Of course, we admire morality. But there's another side to the coin; we also dislike it, because, by its superior standards, we show up so poorly. If we admire a saint, we're also quick to martyr him. "I never go to church," boasted a lord to Bishop Hereford, "because there are so many hypocrites there." "Don't let that keep you away," came the reply. "There's always room for one more." The genuinely religious individual bespeaks a life of discipline, a life of deep values, a life fed by something other than materialism. The real religious individual, he's an enviable person, a superior kind of human being. No wonder there are many who don't like him and are very anxious to paint him as a hypocrite. Down deep, they're jealous of him, of what he stands for. More than that, down deep they see in him a commentary on their own failures, a painful challenge. So they proceed to dislike him.

No one can really blame Joseph's brothers for being envious of him and are very anxious to paint him as a hypocrite. Down deep censure them for their envy, but, rather, for allowing it to grow into enmity. This is the crucial mandate—not to eradicate our jealousy, that's impossible; but to learn to live with it.

March, 1958

THE ADVANTAGES OF SELF-CRITICISM

Folk sayings have a way of embracing a great deal of practical wisdom and affording the most rewarding kind of counsel. That is why the learned Sages of the Talmud were not, as sometimes intellectuals superciliously tend to be, beyond paying heed to the popular maxims of their day. From time to time, they would commend a particular sententious saying to our serious attention, and even enhance its validity by investing it with Biblical confirmation. One such folk proverb that caught their fancy had to do with the phenomenon of self-criticism. "If there is any matter of reproach in you, be you yourself the first to tell it." The Rabbis underscored the desirability of this popular admonition, and lent it the prestige of Scriptural corroboration by pointing to Eliezer, the servant of Abraham, who unsolicitedly volunteered detractive information about his own person.

In our own idiom, we'd phrase it something like this—it's better to jump the gun and criticize yourself than to wait for others to criticize you. Better for a number of cogent reasons. Surely everyone will allow that there isn't a person on earth who is so perfect that he is clear of all fault and not blameworthy of one thing or another at one time or other. We are all legitimate targets of criticism. Yet, it's so very hard to take criticism. "Of all the cants which are canted in this canting world, the cant of criticism is the most tormenting," said Lawrence Sterne. If, then, take it we must, we can at least palliate its harshness by taking it from ourselves. We take our strictures more graciously when they come from ourselves.

It's wiser to anticipate criticism and declare our own faults, because, in that manner, we safeguard our relationships and abort the birth of enmities. There are some inordinately fair-minded and impartial individuals to whom the truth is paramount and who,

217

therefore, retain their equanimity and eschew anger even in the face of the most trying censure. Most of us, however, are made of leaner stuff. No matter how good a friend we might regard him, let him make an adverse observation about us, and something of hostility invades our erstwhile feelings towards him. Regardless of how justified they may be in their animadversions, people, in our now hurt sight, become less than our friends, perhaps even our enemies, when they criticize us. Thus, says the proverb, why wait and imperil your friendships; jump the gun and acknowledge your deficiencies.

Self-criticism has another distinct advantage. Criticism that issues from ourselves is more apt to do some good by eventuating in a constructive response. For when it comes from an outside source, what is the normal reaction? Our first reaction, almost inevitably, is to defend ourselves. We build up a defense—we lie and deny, we improvise extenuating circumstances, we fabricate excuses, we rationalize away our culpability. And in our anxiety to protect ourselves, the criticism loses its potential value. It defeats its own purpose. Indeed, ironically enough, it only entrenches us all the more deeply and stubbornly in our faults. When, however, the voice of correction stems from our own persons, there is no occasion for such costly defensive mechanics, and the chances are inestimably better for results of a more positive and effective nature. "A man should never be ashamed to own he has been in the wrong," said Pope. "Which is saying in other words that he is wiser today than he was yesterday."

Is it a fatuous and futile thought that now crosses my naive and impractical preacher's mind? I'm wondering if world hostility would not be reduced, and if better results would not be achieved in the area of international relationships, were it the practice to spend the opening weeks of every U.N. session in a kind of convocation of self-criticism instead of in an orgy of mutual recrimination. But that surely is only a dream, distilled by an ancient heritage, the glory of whose Prophetic and Rabbinic moulders was the boldness of self-criticism. "The self-critical spirit of the Jews is one of the strangest phenomena in history," writes Maurice Samuel.

There are less grandiose realms, however, where such thinking need not be so illusory, as on the level of our personal everyday living. Minister and congregant, too, teacher and student alike, husband as well as wife, employer no less than employee—all of us everywhere can reap much richer rewards from our relationships, if we are wise enough to jump the gun and criticize ourselves before others are compelled to level the charge at us.

November, 1957

ON BEING A BLESSING

It's a catchy phrase, and no little enigmatic, too. "Be thou a blessing," the Patriarch Abraham is enjoined by the Lord. Somehow or other, the noun "blessing" doesn't seem to square with the verb "to be." One bestows a blessing, one works it, one provides it; but how can one be a blessing? What kind of a blessing is it that issues not from giving, not from doing and working, but just from sheer being?

When one ponders it a bit, there is such a phenomenon. Sometimes it's not what you do, or say, or give; it's just your being there that is a blessing. Job's friends meant so well. When they heard of all the evil that had befallen poor Job, they came to visit and comfort him. To bring him solace, each of the three, in his own way, spoke at length to him, seeking to explain his misfortune and provide a rationale for his suffering. But the more they indulged in explications, the more they managed to discomfort him and aggravate his misery. Job's comforters! They did well to visit with him. But that's all they should have done. Not to talk, not to philosophize, not to justify his wretchedness—far better would it have been just to be there and let him talk.

Just to be there, that's all. Not only in an hour of adversity but in so many different instances, sometimes it is precisely our passivity that is such a blessing. The human lot is such that there are times when each of us has something to get off his chest. We have to unburden and we desperately need somebody to listen to us. We don't want anything from him, and we may even know that he can't help us; all we need is someone to be with us, someone to talk to. I am in no way denigrating the psychiatrist's work when I aver that there are times when the help he brings is effectuated by just being there and listening, and that's all. This was the vein of a woman's problem in my study the other week. She realized that

220

there was nothing her husband could do about many of her complaints and woes. In fact, she really didn't expect him to do anything about them. All she wanted—and this she didn't get from him—was for him to be around more often to listen to her. Often, sheer presence can be the greatest of blessings.

Think of this idea of being a blessing in this light, too—frequently it's not the goodness you do, but rather the kind of person you are that distils the blessing. Prayed the little girl who felt she had been unjustly disciplined by her parents, "O Lord, please make all the bad people good; and Lord, if it's possible, please make all the good people nice." It's a disconcerting paradox. Even when we do the right thing, sometimes we're not quite nice.

We can contribute to a cause, perhaps even handsomely, but then rob the beneficence of the generosity with the cynicism of our persons. It's a prevalent phenomenon in family life. We're unstinting providers. Thanks to our means and liberality, wife and children have every benefit and enjoy every advantage. But is that enough? Some of the greatest unhappiness and discontent reside in the most luxurious dwellings and in the freest spending families. Giving is not yet a blessing; more important, one has to be nice. Who was it that remarked, "Some women work so hard to make good husbands that they never quite manage to make good wives"? All praise to the conscientious housewife and hail the solicitous mother. But when all is said and done, it's not how much she does and achieves for her family, it's the kind of person she is in their midst that confers blessing upon the home. And how true it is in my own realm, too. It boots little blessing if an individual observes his faith diligently and piously, and yet in his own person, as a human being, doesn't quite pass muster.

It is said that everyone can bring happiness to others. Some of us do it just by walking into a room; some of us, just by walking out of a room. Where do we belong? Are we, merely by virtue of our own being, a blessing?

February, 1965

WISDOM FOR SERENITY

One of the great quests of all of us is the search for that inner quiet more popularly known as peace of mind. In spite of all the inadequacies of this latter phrase, it is, in a sense, a most felicitous designation. For peace of mind is a serenity than can be acquired only through the exercise of wisdom and understanding; it's the compensation of a kind of philosophy of life.

The wisdom to understand, in the first instance, that tranquility is not synonymous with an untroubled existence. A completely content and worry-free life is an impossibility and sheer fiction. The appetitive aspect of our human nature can never be fully satisfied. Nor can we eschew the overwhelming fact that much of man's destiny is governed by circumstances and conditions beyond his control. Professor Abraham Heschel defined life itself as concern. All this does not imply, however, that peace is unattainable. On the contrary, it is only when we demand the impossible and expect the fatuous, when we rebel against the inevitables, that we become most tragically disturbed and rack our beings with futile torment. Start with a philosophy of realism—to paraphrase a Rabbinic dictum, acquiesce to the human lot—and you will be graced with a rewarding measure of calm and inner composure.

There is a tendency in these times of know-how to evaluate a person in terms of success. It is a victimizing criterion, for by its insatiable standards there is scarcely a person who has reason for contentment and is not a failure. To restore a sense of inner peace, it is essential to replace our philosophy of success with a philosophy of effort, to operate on the conviction that achievement is not nearly as important as honest trying. There is much comfort that issues from the knowledge that, though we did not succeed, we at least did our best; a saving relief from the bitter barbs of remorse to feel that, in spite of the results, we on our part were not found wanting.

We need, too, the wisdom to perceive that serenity is the concomitant of simple living. There is no doubt that many a person unnecessarily complicates what might have been a comfortable existence with white elephants born of social vanity, overreaching ambition, and the pursuit of the glamorous and the exciting. Perspicacity cautions that the game is not always worth the candle, and that abiding benefit can accrue from scaling down the pace.

Frequently it is our own disingenuousness that gets in the way of peace of mind. There is a market-mentality in our society that has us selling even ourselves through all the externals and wiles of salesmanship. Sincerity becomes secondary to showmanship, and the ability to impress people is at a higher premium than inner substance and worth. It is the same tenor that has hypocrisized decency by reducing it to the shallow level of mere propriety. But there's the rub. We might even fool all the people all the time, but ultimately we can't fool ourselves without damaging our equanimity. We can't push personality at the cost of character, pretense at the price of essence, and enjoy inner peace. For serenity, whatever else it needs, requires the soil of honesty and genuineness, the philosophy of being a real person.

Finally, we need the wisdom to understand that there can be no peace in life without Religion. When all is said and done, there is a spiritual dimension in man, and you can't starve this dimension without seriously impairing the balance and serenity of the human being. In spite of the postulates of scientific positivism, man is, willy-nilly, bothered by the big questions which comprise the preoccupation of Faith. You can no more deprive him of metaphysics than you can of food and then expect contentment. Without a religious *weltanschauung,* as the experience of the modern period so vividly confirms, man simply can't find peace. And is it not Religion, too, with its unparalleled inculcation of ethical and moral living, that affords us the most practical and effective armor against those deviations which inevitably destroy our serenity? Nor can we overlook the overwhelming fact that, of all our modern systems, it is Faith alone that underscores the doctrines of forgiveness and another chance, tenets which are so indispensable to the inner peace of the frail human creature.

Perhaps we can never achieve complete peace of mind—perfection is always beyond our grasp. But surely we can acquire a measure great enough to cause us to sing with the Psalmist: "He leadeth me beside the waters of serenity."

January, 1956